TREASURES IN THE SMITHSONIAN

The Gem Collection

Paul E. Desautels
Curator, Division of Mineralogy

Photography by Dane Penland

Smithsonian Institution Press   Washington, D.C.   1979

Copyright 1979 by Smithsonian Institution. All rights reserved.

Library of Congress Cataloging in Publication Data

Desautels, Paul E
Treasures in the Smithsonian: the gem collection.
1. Gems. 2. Smithsonian Institution. I. Smithsonian Institution. II. Title.
NK5510.W3D43 736'.2'0740153 79-16475
ISBN 0-87474-360-5
ISBN 0-87474-361-3 pbk.

Frontispiece: One of the more important gifts to the Smithsonian gem collection in recent years is the 68-carat Victoria-Transvaal diamond set in a flattering gold and diamond necklace. Given by Mr. and Mrs. Leonard Wilkinson, this dazzling, champagne-colored gem was discovered in Africa in 1951.

The Gem Collection

CONTENTS

- I. THE NATIONAL GEM COLLECTION   7
- II. THE STUDY OF GEMS   10
- III. THE SHAPING OF GEMSTONES   16
- IV. GEM SUBSTITUTES   24
- V. GEM LORE   27
- VI. PRINCIPAL GEM SPECIES   29

    Diamond   29
    Corundum: Includes Ruby and Sapphire   32
    Beryl: Includes Emerald and Aquamarine   33
    Pearl   37
    Topaz   40
    Opal   40
    Spinel   44
    Quartz: Includes Rock Crystal, Amethyst, and Citrine   44
    Chrysoberyl: Includes Alexandrite and Cat's-eye   48
    Tourmaline   49
    Zircon   52
    Peridot   53
    Spodumene   53
    Garnet   56
    Jade   60
    Gemstones for the Collector   60

- VII. JEWELRY   64
- VIII. GEMS IN THE COLLECTION   66

A partial view of the Hall of Gems, which houses the National Collection of Gems in the National Museum of Natural History.

Directly opposite the entrance to the Hall of Gems, a special vault houses the Hope diamond, the single most popular object in the Museum.

I. THE NATIONAL GEM COLLECTION

Man has been using certain mineral species for personal adornment since prehistoric times. However, of approximately 3,000 different mineral species known, relatively few, perhaps only 100, have been used traditionally as gems. To be useful as a gem, a mineral species should have durability as well as beauty. Lack of durability eliminates many minerals as gems, although some relatively fragile gem materials, such as opal, are prized because of their exceptional beauty. Actually, some gem materials are technically not minerals at all. Pearl, amber, jet, and coral, unlike true minerals, are derived from living organisms.

In the National Gem Collection, the Smithsonian Institution has assembled, along with the closely related collection of minerals, a large representation of all known gem materials. The display portion of the collection consists of more than 1,000 items selected to illustrate the various kinds of gems and to show how their beauty is enhanced by cutting and polishing. Most of these gems are gifts of public-spirited donors who, by giving the gems directly or by establishing endowments for their purchase, have contributed to the enjoyment of the many thousands of persons who visit the Smithsonian Institution each week.

The National Gem Collection had its beginning in 1884 when Professor F. W. Clarke, then honorary curator of the Division of Mineralogy, prepared an exhibit of American gem stones as a part of the Smithsonian Institution's display at the New Orleans Exposition. The same collection was also displayed at the Cincinnati Exposition the following year. Between 1886 and 1890 the growth of the collection was slow, but in 1891 most of the gems collected by Dr. Joseph Leidy of Philadelphia were obtained. Combined with those already on hand, all were exhibited at the World's Columbian Exposition at Chicago in 1893.

Great stimulus was given the gem collection in 1894 when Mrs. Frances Lea Chamberlain bequeathed to the Smithsonian the precious stones assembled by her father, Dr. Isaac Lea. Her husband, Dr. Leander T. Chamberlain, who in 1897 was appointed honorary curator of the collection, contributed many specimens and, upon his death, left an endowment fund for support of the gem collection. The income from that fund has been used to increase the collection over the years. Following the example of the founders of the gem collection in the last century, a succession of custodians and curators have continued to take an interest in its welfare. Wirt Tassin, assisted by Professor A. S. Eakle, published in 1902 the first catalog of the collection. The second, much expanded catalog, of George P. Merrill, assisted by Margaret Moody and Edgar T. Wherry, appeared in 1922. It was during the occupancy of the building by the War Risk Bureau (October 1917 to March 1919) that the gem collection was totally rearranged and recataloged separately from the mineral collection. Curators William A. Foshag and Edward P. Henderson brought the collection safely through the troublesome years of the Great Depression and World War II. George S. Switzer gave the collection its strongest push into new life in the modern era by arranging for the acquisition of the Hope diamond and by initiating the plans for a new exhibit hall. Building on this strong foundation the present curator, Paul E. Desautels, has brought about the greatest expansion and improvement in the collection that it has had in its history. The change is well documented through the first (1965), second (1972), and third (1979) editions of this publication. Extremely rare and costly gems needed for public exhibit are beyond the income derived from the Chamberlain endowment, but this money shortage has been

Above left: Professor F. W. Clarke, former honorary curator who assembled the Smithsonian's first gem collection in 1884.

Above right: Dr. Isaac Lea, Philadelphia gem collector whose collection was the nucleus around which the present gem collection has been built through the years.

Above left: Dr. Leander T. Chamberlain, son-in-law of Dr. Isaac Lea. He was appointed honorary curator of the gem collection in 1897. Income from his later bequest is now used to purchase gems for the Isaac Lea gem collection.

Above right: Dr. George P. Merrill, former head of the Department of Mineral Sciences whose extensive 1922 catalog of the Smithsonian's gems established the future direction of the collection and stimulated great interest in it.

overcome by many important donations, among the most notable being the gifts in 1959 of the Hope diamond by Harry Winston, Inc., New York City, and of the Victoria-Transvaal diamond by Mr. and Mrs. Leonard Wilkinson in 1977. Thus, from modest beginnings in 1884, there has been accumulated this magnificent collection of gems belonging to the people of the United States. The collection is displayed in the Smithsonian Institution's great National Museum of Natural History.

Above left: Dr. Edward P. Henderson, currently curator emeritus in the Department of Mineral Sciences, maintained the collection during the troublesome years of the Great Depression and during World War II. He is the link between the old and new periods of development of the gem collection.

Above right: Dr. William Foshag, a former department chairman who brought to the Museum the famous Roebling and Canfield mineral collections in 1926. These collections consisted primarily of mineral specimens but also contained a number of superb gems that enriched the gem collection substantially.

Above left: Dr. George Switzer, a former department chairman who had a strong interest in gems and brought the collection into the modern era. His monumental contribution was the acquisition in 1959 of the gem collection's greatest attraction, the Hope diamond.

Above right: Paul E. Desautels, present curator of the gem collection.

II. THE STUDY OF GEMS

To the average shopper it might seem that a jeweler's showcase of gems presents innumerable kinds of precious stones, when actually only very few species of minerals are seen there. Perhaps only diamond, ruby, emerald, aquamarine, sapphire, opal, tourmaline, and amethyst would comprise the entire stock. Yet, since the mineral kingdom consists of a few thousand distinct species, it would seem that more kinds of gemstones would be available. Certainly, many more minerals than are seen displayed by the jeweler have been used as gems over the centuries. The study of all these species of gem minerals constitutes modern gemology—a specialized branch of the science of mineralogy.

With the few exceptions already noted—amber, coral, pearl, and jet—all gems are minerals found in the earth's crust. A mineral species is a natural substance having a definite chemical composition and definite physical characteristics by which it can be recognized and distinguished from others. However, for a mineral to qualify as a gem it must meet at least some of the generally accepted requirements—brilliance, beauty, durability, rarity, and portability, and must have at least some availability. Of course, if a gemstone happens to be "fashionable" it will have additional importance. Rarely does a single kind of gem possess all of these qualities. A fine-quality diamond, having a high degree of brilliance and fire, together with extreme hardness and great rarity, comes closest to this ideal, and in the world of western fashion the diamond is unchallenged among gems. The opal, by contrast, is relatively fragile, and it depends mainly on its rarity and its beautiful play of colors to be prized as a gem material.

When a gem material, as found in nature, has at least a minimum number of these necessary qualities, it is then the task of the lapidary, or gem cutter, to cut and polish it in such a way as to take greatest advantage of all its possibilities for beauty and adornment.

Physical Characteristics of Gemstones

When a gemologist or a gem cutter examines an unworked mineral fragment (called *rough*) he looks for certain distinguishing characteristics that will aid him in identifying the mineral and in determining the procedures he should use in cutting it.

It is difficult to list these characteristics in the order of importance, but *hardness* would rank high. Hardness of a gem is best defined as its resistance to abrasion or scratching. Most commonly used for hardness comparisons is the Mohs scale, which consists of selected common minerals arranged in the order of increasing hardness. On this scale, topaz is rated as 8 in hardness, ruby as 9, and diamond, the hardest known substance, as 10. Any gem with a hardness less than that of quartz, number 7 in the scale, is unlikely to be sufficiently scratch-resistant for use as an important gem. A less precise scale, using common objects for comparison, might include the fingernail with a hardness of 2½, a copper coin up to 3, a knife blade to 5½, a piece of window glass about 5½, and a steel file between 6 and 7, depending on the type of steel. By this scale, any stone that remains unmarred after being scraped by a piece of window glass will have a hardness greater than 5½. The more important gemstones—which include diamond, ruby, sapphire, and emerald—all have a hardness much greater than 5½.

The size of a gem or rough usually is indicated by its *weight* in *carats*. The expression "a 10-carat stone" has meaning—if somewhat inexact—even to the nonexpert. Specifically, a carat is one-fifth of a gram, which is a unit of weight in the metric system small enough so that approximately 28 grams make an ounce. A 140-carat gemstone, then, weighs about an ounce.

Another distinguishing characteristic of a gemstone is its *specific gravity*, which is an expression of the relationship between the stone's own weight and the weight of an equal volume of water. We are aware of a difference in weight when we compare lead and wood, yet it would not always be correct to say that lead weighs more than wood, for a large

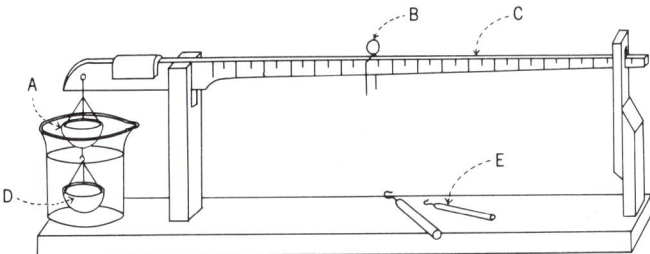

Sketch of a simple balance used to determine the specific gravity of a gemstone. The operator places the gemstone in the upper pan (A), moves the weight (B) along the beam (C) until it balances perfectly, and notes the number at the weight's position. He then transfers the gemstone to the lower pan (D), which is completely immersed in water, and moves the weight along the beam to restore balance. He notes the scale number at the new position and determines the specific gravity simply by dividing the first number by the difference between the two numbers. If the gemstone is large, the operator can use heavier sliding weights (E).

Traces of iron impurities in this agate, and its slow formation in a rock cavity, have produced a beautifully colored and distinctive pattern which instantly tells the gem enthusiast that this sample came from a deposit in Bruno Canyon, Owyhee County, Idaho.

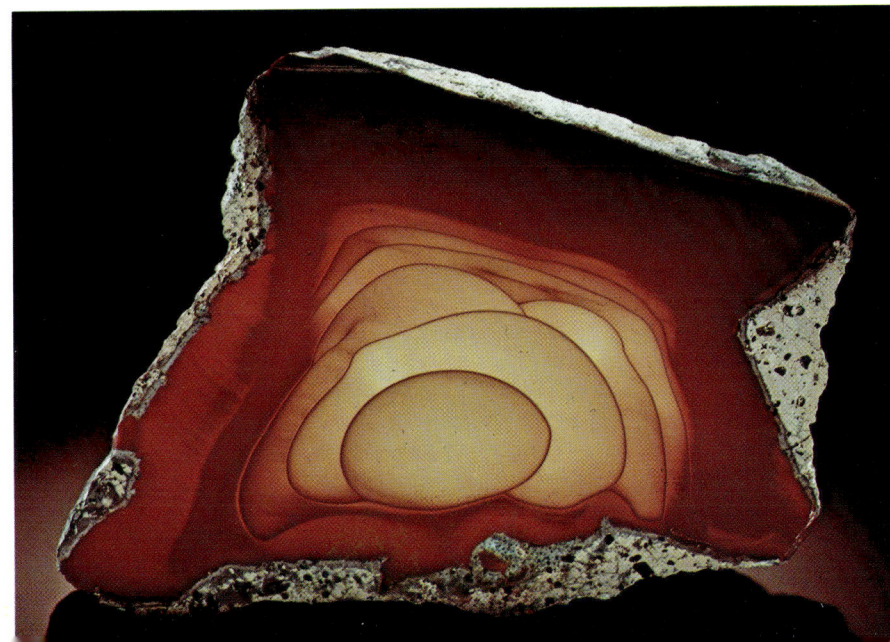

piece of wood can weigh more than a small piece of lead. Only by comparing equal volumes of these minerals can the extent of the weight difference be clear and unmistakable. Diamond is 3½ times heavier than the same volume of water, so its specific gravity is 3½. Since each species of gem has its own specific gravity, which can easily be determined without harming the stone, this standard of comparison is a valuable aid in identifying gems. Several techniques have been devised for determining specific gravity, and most of them make use of some kind of weighing device or balance.

Among the most striking and useful of the distinguishing characteristics of gemstones are those that involve their effects on light.

An important effect of a gem on light is the production of color, upon which many gems depend for their beauty. Some gem materials, such as lapis lazuli, have little to offer except color. Many of the major gem minerals vary widely in color, owing to the presence of finely dispersed impurities in extremely small quantities. Traces of iron in the composition of a gem can produce shades of green, red, brown, yellow, blue, or black. Chromium gives rise to tints of green, violet, red, and yellow. Manganese, titanium, uranium, and several other elements are among the coloring agents. Thus, the gemstone beryl may occur as blue green (aquamarine), as pink (morganite), as rich green (emerald), as yellow (heliodor), or even colorless (goshenite).

Gemstones such as beryl and sapphire that depend on impurities for their color are said to be *allochromatic;* others, such as peridot and garnet, which are highly colored even when pure, are said to be *idiochromatic.* The color of a gem is further described according to its *hue, tint,* and *intensity.* Hue refers to the kind of color, such as red, yellow, green; tint refers to the lightness or darkness of the hue; and intensity refers to vividness or dullness. Throughout history, the most popular colored stones have been those with hues of red, green, or blue of dark tint and high intensity.

The effect of a gem on light may be more than the production of color. Several of the so-called phenomenal stones are prized for other effects. Holes, bubbles, and foreign particles, when properly aligned in parallel groupings, can produce interesting light effects. The play of colors of opal and labradorite; the *chatoyancy,* or silky sheen, of tiger's-eye and cat's-eye; the *opalescence,* or pearly reflections, of opal and moonstone; and the *asterism,* or star effect, of rubies and sapphires are caused by the reaction of light to accumulations of minute *inclusions* or imperfections in the gemstone.

When light passes into or through a gemstone with little or no interruption, the stone is said to be transparent. A stone through which light passes with greater difficulty is said to be either translucent or opaque, depending on the degree of light interruption.

Frequently, the internal structure of a gem acts as a filter, permitting only certain kinds of light to pass through. When all kinds are transmitted, the gem appears white or colorless. Otherwise it assumes the hue of the color transmitted. Strikingly, some gems will transmit different colors depending on the direction in the stone along which light passes. This phenomenon is known as *pleochroism* and is often quite noticeable in tanzanite, kunzite, and cordierite.

The action of a gemstone upon the light that strikes its surface, and is either reflected or passed through it, sometimes results in other highly desirable effects that enhance the stone's beauty and aid in its identification. Light passing into a stone is bent from its path, and the amount of bending *(refraction)* depends upon the species of the gemstone. When the degree of bending can be measured, the gem species can be identified, since very few species of gemstones bend light to exactly the same degree. An instrument called a gem refractometer is used to determine the degree to which cut stones refract, or bend, light. The measurement obtained is the *refractive index* of the gemstone.

Many gemstones can split a beam of light and bend one part more than the other, thus producing *double refraction,* or two different measurements of refractive index.

Some gems have the ability to separate "white light" (the mixture of all colors) into its various colors, producing flashes of red, yellow, green, and other colors. Separation occurs because the various colors, or wavelengths composing white light passing through the gem, are each bent or refracted a different amount. Red is bent least, followed in order by orange, yellow, green, blue, and violet, which is bent most. This characteristic of being able to produce flashes of color, as seen prominently in diamond, is known as *dispersion* or *fire*. Quartz and glass have low dispersion, and hence, they make poor diamond substitutes. Some of the newer synthetic gemstones, such as YAG, GGG, and cubic zirconia, have extremely high dispersion, with resulting fire. Zircon, a natural gemstone of suitable hardness, exhibits suitably high dispersion and has been a commonly used substitute for diamond.

Chemical Characteristics of Gemstones

Since gems are embraced in the mineral kingdom, and minerals are naturally occurring chemical substances, it follows that all the accepted terms of chemical description can be applied to them. When a chemist learns that ruby is an impure aluminum oxide, he understands a great deal about the nature, origin, and behavior of ruby. He can assign to it the chemical formula Al_2O_3, symbolizing its basic composition as two atoms of aluminum united with three of oxygen. Similarly, other popular gemstones can be described chemically as follows:

Diamond	Carbon	C
Sapphire	Aluminum oxide	Al_2O_3
Quartz	Silicon dioxide	SiO_2
Emerald	Beryllium aluminum silicate	$Be_3Al_2(SiO_3)_6$
Spinel	Magnesium aluminate	$Mg(AlO_2)_2$

Significantly, ruby and sapphire are chemically identical, both being of the mineral species corundum. As already explained, the difference in color is due entirely to very slight traces of chemical impurities. Frequently, the impurities are present in irregular patches that give spotty color effects.

Some mineral species possess many of the desirable qualities of gemstones, yet cannot be used as gems because they are chemically active and therefore are less durable. They undergo alteration and decomposition when exposed to light or to one or another of such substances as air, water, skin acids, and oils. With very few exceptions all the better known gems are mineral oxides or silicates. A few oxides, such as corundum, chrysoberyl, and spinel, are remarkably durable. Most silicates—substances containing the elements silicon and oxygen in their compositions—are, on the other hand, generally resistant to alteration and decomposition, unlike the sulfides, carbonates, and most other mineral groups. One notable exception to the rule is carbon, which occurs as the extremely durable diamond.

Asterism, resulting from the light reflection of three sets of needlelike inclusions arrayed at 60-degree angles to each other—as they are in this quartz sphere from New Hampshire—has the same origin in star gems of sapphire, ruby, and others.

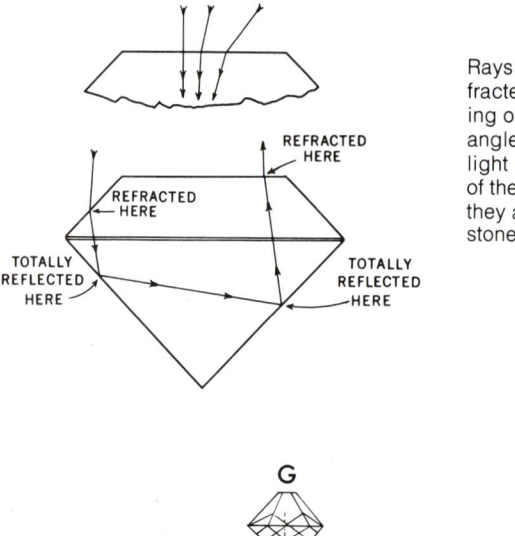

Rays of light passing into a gemstone are refracted (bent) in varying amounts depending on the gem species and also on the angle at which the light strikes the stone. The light rays are reflected back toward the top of the stone by internal faces (facets), and they are refracted again as they leave the stone.

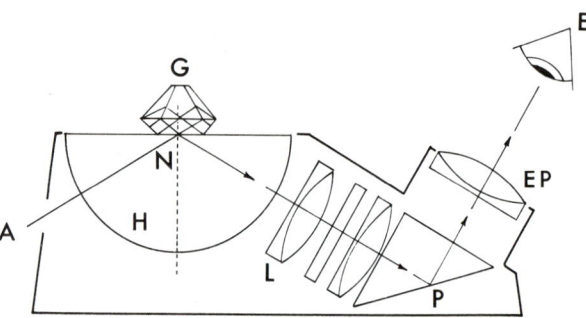

A gem refractometer is a simple device used to measure quickly the refractive index of a cut gemstone. When a beam of light is passed through the opening (A), it is reflected from the table of a gemstone (G) through a lens system (L) and, by prism (P), into the eye of the observer (E). The maximum angle of reflection (N), which depends on the refractive index of the gemstone, controls the angle at which the beam comes through the eyepiece (EP). The refractive index is read directly from a scale in the eyepiece.

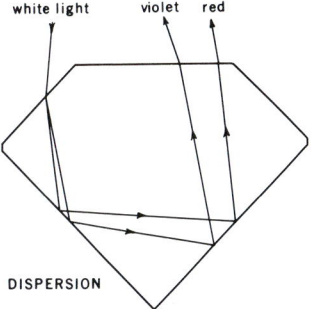

When a ray of ordinary white light enters some gemstones it is dispersed (split up) into rays of the separate colors of which it is composed. These rays are reflected inside the gem and are further separated by additional refraction as they leave the gemstone. This dispersion accounts for the colored flashes of light, or fire, for which diamonds are highly prized.

This 16.7-carat, brilliant-cut diamond, a gift of Mrs. G. Burton Pearson, clearly exhibits the brilliance and especially the color flashes from dispersion that are expected of high-quality, well-cut diamonds.

III. THE SHAPING OF GEMSTONES

Gemstone crystals often have naturally brilliant, reflecting faces, but rarely are they perfect and unblemished. Also, these natural shapes do not provide the best expression of luster, brilliance, dispersion, color, and other inherent properties. In fashioning a gemstone, the skilled artisan tries to develop these hidden assets of the mineral species and to otherwise enhance the gemstone's general beauty.

From ancient times until the 1600s little was attempted in the way of shaping gemstones other than to smooth or polish the natural form. Although similarly smoothed, or *tumbled,* gemstones recently have returned to fashion, the finest pieces of gem rough are now converted mainly into *faceted,* or shaped, stones. Standard types of facets—the flat faces that are ground and polished on the rough gem material—have been given individual and group names. A typical example is the *brilliant* cut, which is most commonly used to best bring out the qualities of a diamond.

The diagram shows a brilliant-cut diamond with angles and facets arranged to give the stone maximum internal reflection, as well as to make use of its strong dispersive ability. Certain of the light beams passing into

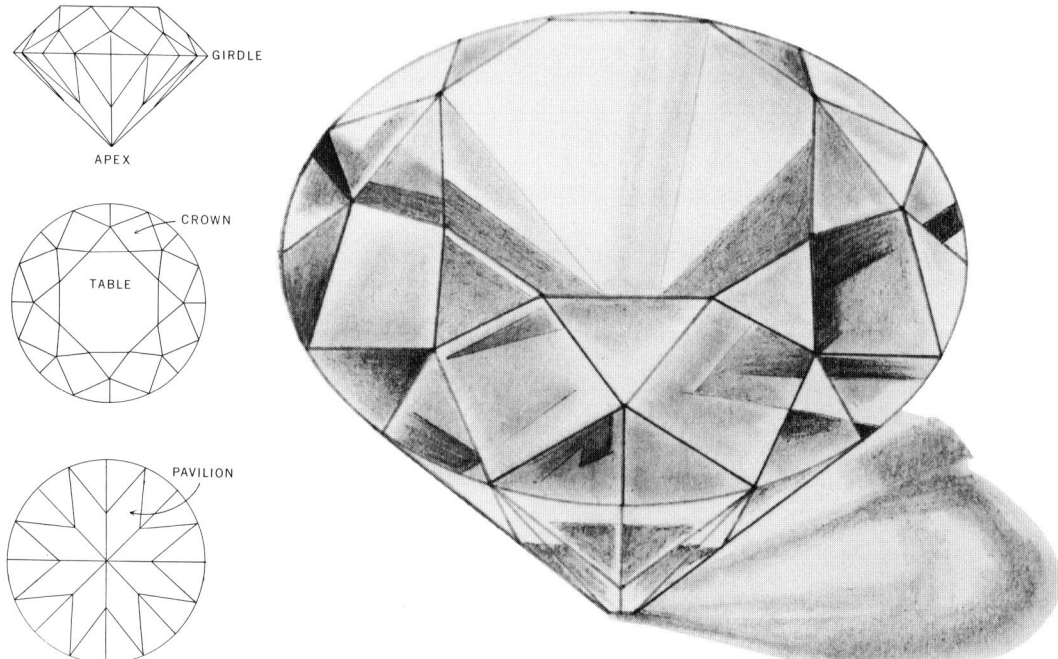

Above left: Characteristic of the standard brilliant cut are the thirty-two crown facets surrounding a relatively small, flat, table facet and the twenty-four pavilion facets and culet at the bottom of the stone.

Above right: The standard brilliant cut, with its pattern of many facets, is commonly used for gemstones having a high refractive index and, therefore, great brilliance.

a brilliant-cut diamond produce colorless brilliance by being reflected back out of the stone through the *table* by which they entered. Other light beams, emerging through inclined facets, are split up by dispersion into the rainbow, or fire, effect so prized in diamonds. A stone that has been cut too wide for its depth, with incorrect facet angles, will look large for its weight, but its brilliance and fire will have been drastically reduced.

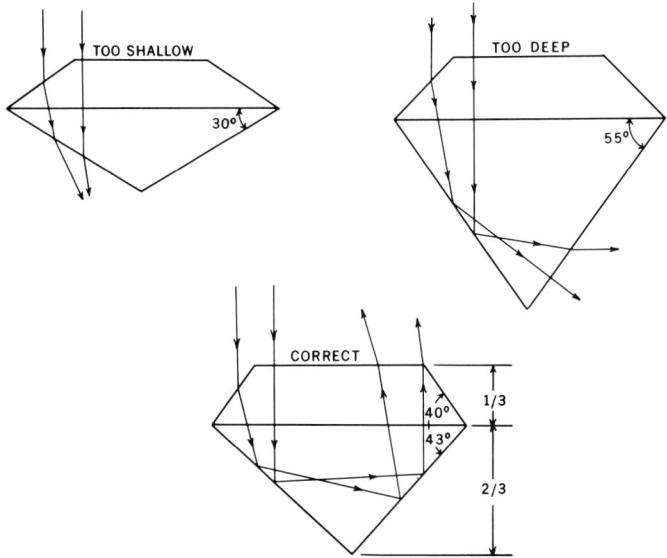

Ideal proportions for the standard brilliant cut have been carefully determined so that the maximum amount of light will be reflected back out the top of the stone. Incorrect proportions cause the light to be lost at the bottom of the stone.

For other purposes and for other kinds of precious stones, a number of basic cuts have been developed. The *brilliant* and *step* cuts are by far the commonest of these basic cuts, but modern jewelry design frequently uses such fancy cuts as the baguette, cut-corner triangle, epaulet, half moon, hexagon, keystone, kite, lozenge, marquise, pentagon, square, trapeze, and triangle. Some of these are shown here.

In general, there are three operations in preparing a gemstone from the rough—sawing, grinding, and polishing. Sawing usually is accomplished by using a thin, diamond-impregnated, rapidly rotating disk of soft iron or bronze, with oil or water being used as a coolant. The very hard diamond dust literally scratches its way through the stone. Once the stone is sawed to shape, the facets are ground and polished on a rotating horizontal disk by the use of various abrasives. For rough grinding, silicon carbide—or sometimes diamond powder—is used. Scratches are removed and a high polish is given by the use of tin oxide, pumice, rouge, or other fine-grained abrasives. The thick disks, or *laps,* are made of cast iron, copper, lead, pewter, wood, cloth, leather, and certain other materials. Since each species of gemstone differs in its characteristics, each must be treated somewhat differently as to sawing and lapping speeds, kind of lap, and choice of abrasives. Because of the greatly increased interest in gem cutting as a hobby and the large number of amateur cutters, a substantial market has developed in the United States for lapidary supplies and equipment. New kinds of machinery, new abrasives, and new kinds of saws and laps are introduced regularly. Fundamentally, however, the process still involves sawing, grinding, and polishing.

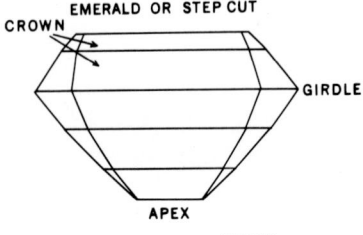

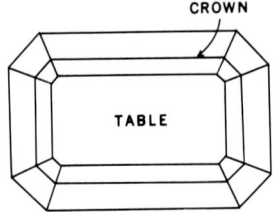

The emerald or step cut provides a large table and a full bottom for the stone. Although the number of crown facets and pavilion facets may vary, the general pattern is maintained.

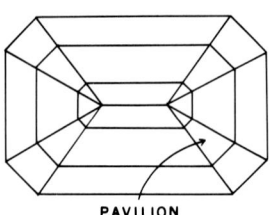

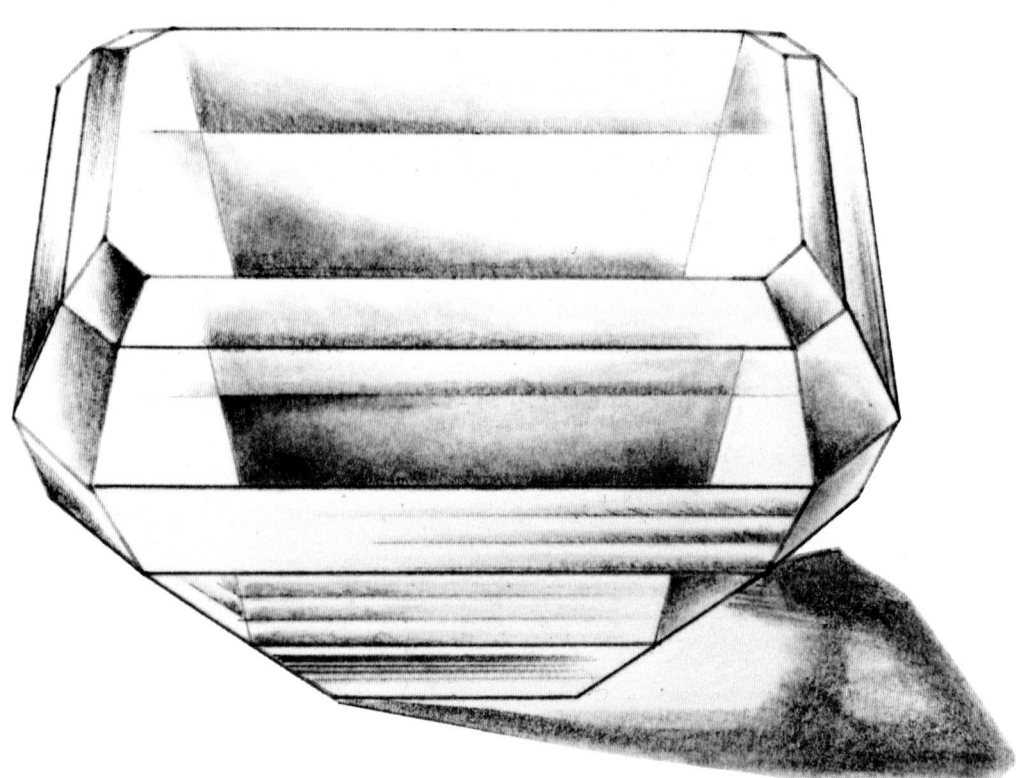

The step cut, often called the emerald cut, frequently is used for colored stones because the large table facet permits a good view of the internal color.

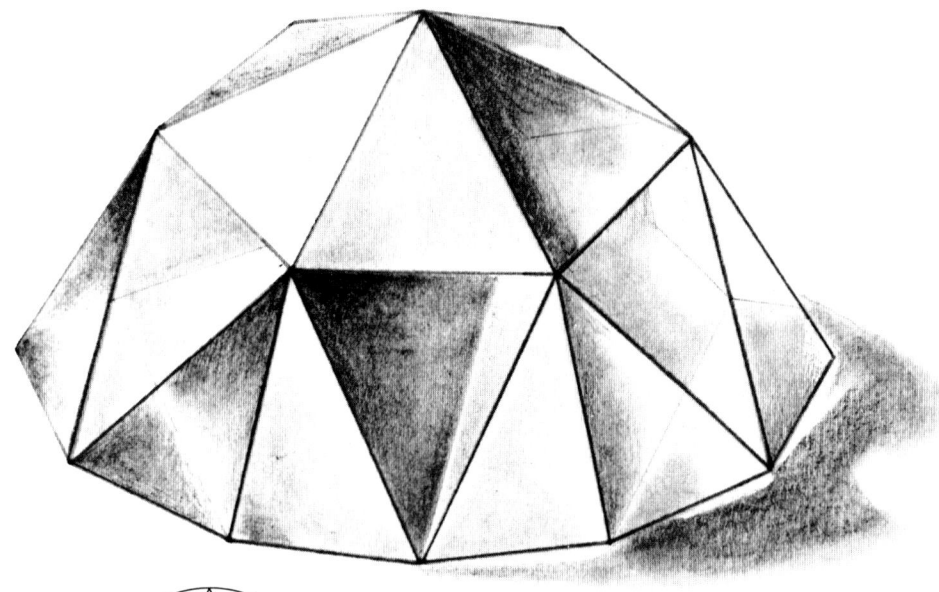

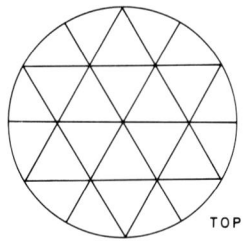

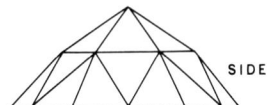

The Dutch rose cut is a very simple one that was used mainly for small diamonds in older jewelry featuring a larger, colored stone. It is based on a form that originated in India and was introduced through Venice.

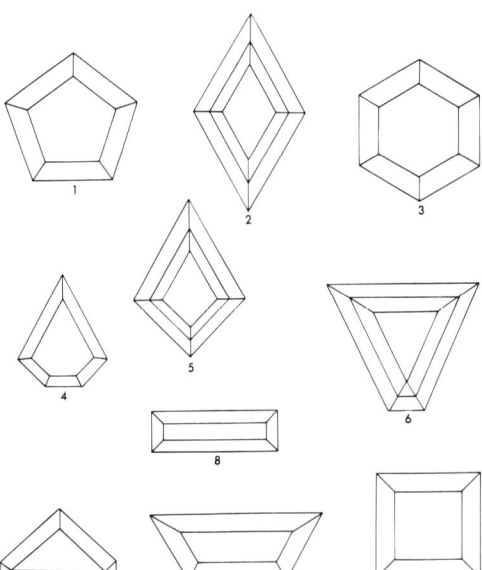

Various kinds of cuts have been devised for special purposes in jewelry design. These include the pentagon (1), lozenge (2), hexagon (3), cut-corner triangle (4), kite (5), keystone (6), epaulet (7), baguette (8), trapeze (9), and square (10).

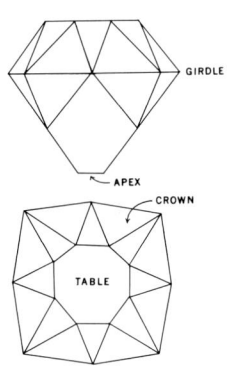

The simplified English brilliant cut takes maximum advantage of the strong dispersion of diamond, with its flashes of fire, but the fewer facets provide less sparkle than the standard brilliant cut.

The English brilliant cut has twenty-eight crown and pavilion facets—twenty-eight fewer than the standard brilliant cut.

Shaping of gemstones is not limited to geometric faceting. Many stones, especially those that are opaque or produce stars and cat's-eyes, are cut as *cabochons*. The ancient, and probably oldest, cutting style consists merely of a raised and rounded form. When extended completely around the stone, the cabochon form results in a bead that can be drilled and strung. Many cabochons, especially those of less expensive gem materials, are now cut in large quantities to standard sizes in order to fit mass-produced gem mountings.

Sculpting in gemstones is a much more intricate, nongeometric kind of shaping. Although tools differ in detail, and the gem sculptor must possess an artistic eye as well as lapidary skill, the basic processes of sawing, grinding, and polishing are the same.

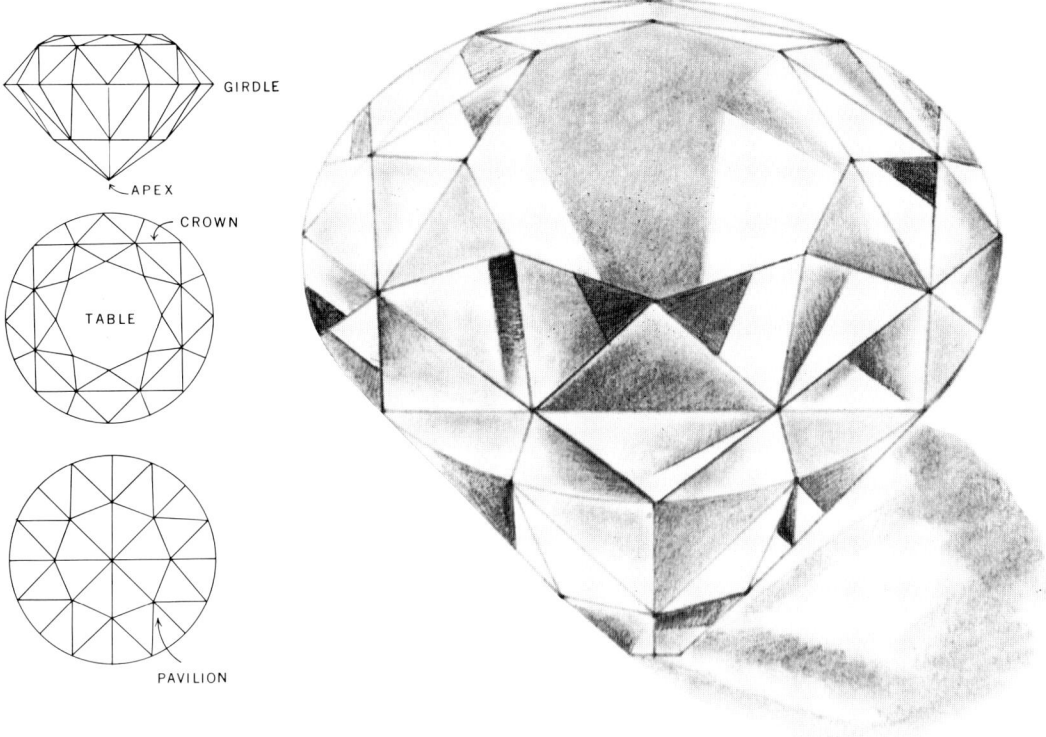

The step brilliant cut is a complicated modification of the standard brilliant. With an additional twelve facets in the crown and eight in the pavilion, the step brilliant has seventy-eight facets as compared with the fifty-eight of the standard. Just as the English brilliant cut, because of its twenty-eight fewer facets, has less sparkle than the standard brilliant cut, the step brilliant, with its twenty additional facets, has greater sparkle.

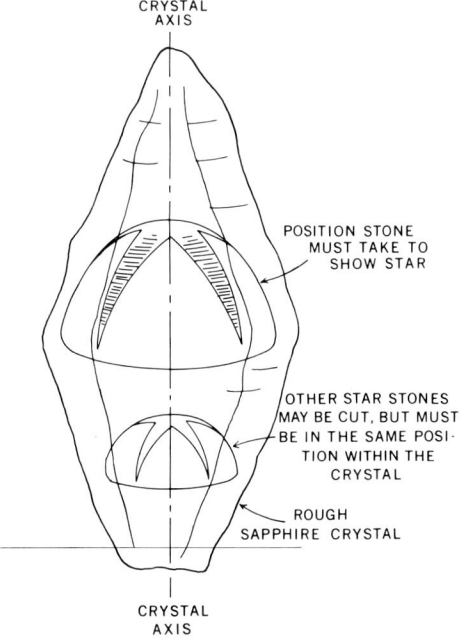

Cutting a star stone requires careful attention to the directions in which the cuts are to be made. Failure to align the stone properly with the axis of the crystal will produce a stone with an off-center, crooked, or dim star, or may even eliminate the star completely.

Part of a large set of three- to four-inch bowls carved of American gem materials by George Ashley of California. Clockwise from top left these are Oregon agate, Wyoming jade, Utah variscite, Arizona petrified wood, and Arizona chrysocolla in quartz.

A two-foot ivory piece carved in China from a fossil mammoth tusk. Part of the design resulted from the removal of parts of the tusk that had decomposed through the ages.

These interestingly patterned polished agate cabochons were cut from materials found (left to right) in Oregon, California, Idaho, and Washington.

Carved 2½-inch coral fish of fine color amid branches of uncarved natural coral.

IV. GEM SUBSTITUTES

Because of their rarity and relatively high cost, the number of real gems used throughout recorded time must be insignificant compared to the number of gem substitutes used. There are records of glass and ceramic imitations of gems as early as 3,000 B.C. Certainly, the world gem markets today are flooded with substitutes and man-made gems. There even has been developed a laboratory process for growing a coating of synthetic emerald on the surface of a faceted stone of natural colorless beryl. The recut gem then looks like a natural emerald, and it has natural inclusions that totally synthetic emeralds lack.

In general, gem substitutes can be classified as imitation stones, assembled stones, reconstructed and altered stones, and synthetic stones.

Imitation Stones

Any material will serve as an imitation of a natural gem as long as it resembles the real thing under casual examination. Because of the great variety in types and colors available, glass and plastics are the most commonly used materials for making imitation gems. Almost every gem, even opal, has been simulated effectively. Opal, which has resisted successful imitation for so long, has been recently well simulated in a special kind of glass marketed as Opal Essence. The substitutes offer no difficulty of identification to the expert, but many are deceptive to the layman.

Assembled Stones

It has been the practice for centuries to build up gemstones by fusing or cementing a shaped piece of natural gemstone to another piece, or other pieces, of inferior or artificial material.

A colorless, common beryl crown cemented to a pavilion of green glass produces an emerald-looking doublet—part natural, part artificial—of good color and high durability. A thin piece of beautifully colored opal cemented to a base of inferior opal provides an assembled stone that looks like a thick piece of high-quality opal. Topped by a layer of colorless quartz, the gem is much more durable than unprotected opal. Even stones in which there are pockets of colored liquids, or metal foil between the shaped pieces, are known.

Usually, assembled stones are easily detected, since the joint will show under magnification, but sometimes these assemblages are mounted in settings that obscure the joint, and detection is more difficult.

Reconstructed and Altered Stones

Ruby fragments are reported to have been heated at high temperature to melt them partially to form a larger mass that could be cut into a more

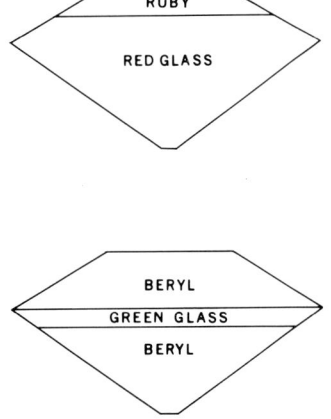

Samples of assembled imitation gemstone. If measured on its natural ruby table, this assembled stone would have all the characteristics of a large ruby, including refractive index. Since emerald is green beryl, an inexpensive colorless beryl sandwich of green glass would appear to be an expensive emerald. The joints of such assembled stones are often hidden in the jewelry mountings.

valuable stone. Ruby and amber are the only materials that have been somewhat successfully reconstituted in this way, but there are many other ways of tampering with natural stones to make them more desirable.

Sometimes natural stones are backed with foil or a metallic coating to enhance their color, to provide brilliance, or to produce a star effect. It is said that in an inventory years ago of the Russian crown jewels by the Soviet Government, the ruby-colored Paul the First diamond was discovered to be a pale pink diamond backed by red foil. Today, some diamonds are coated on the back with a thin blue film to improve their color.

Aquamarine, when pale greenish blue, may be heated in order to deepen the blue color, and poorly colored amethyst may be heated to produce a beautiful yellow-brown quartz, called citrine, that often is misrepresented as topaz. By strong heating, the brown and reddish brown colors of zircon can be changed to blue or colorless, both states unknown in natural zircon. Dyes, plastics, and oils are used to impregnate porous gems such as turquoise and variscite, and even jade. Off-color diamonds, when exposed to strong atomic radiation, can be changed to attractive green, brown, and yellow colors, causing them to resemble higher-priced *fancies*. In recent times beautiful permanent-blue topaz has been introduced, given its fine color by irradiation.

In the constant search for something new, gem suppliers sometimes introduce into gemstones colors that are not always an improvement. For example, the beautiful purple of some amethyst can be converted, by heat treatment, to a peculiar green. Such an altered stone has been marketed as *greened amethyst*.

All of this tampering with gemstones complicates the problem of identifications, so it is a matter of serious concern to the commercial gem trade.

Synthetic Stones

For more than 200 years mineralogists have been devising techniques for producing synthetic minerals in the laboratory, and attempts have been made, sometimes with considerable success, to apply these techniques to the production of synthetic gemstones. To qualify as a synthetic gemstone the man-made product must be identical, chemically and structurally, with its natural counterpart. Sapphire, ruby, spinel, emerald, rutile, and others, in gem quality, have been brought to commercial production.

Two of the basic techniques used in producing synthetic gems are the *flame-fusion* and the *hydrothermal* processes.

In the flame-fusion process—invented in 1904 by the French chemist Verneuil—powdered aluminum oxide, containing coloring agents, is sieved down through the flame of a vertical blowtorch furnace. As it passes through the flame, the powder melts and accumulates as drops on an adjustable stand just below the flame, where it forms a single crystal *boule* of the synthetic rough. In a few hours a boule of several hundred carats can be formed. When such furnaces are operated in banks of several hundred units, the commercial production of corundum alone becomes possible at the rate of many tons a year. Through the years, of course, refinements have been made on Verneuil's original furnace.

In the hydrothermal process, which differs greatly from Verneuil's flame-fusion process, crystals are grown from solutions of the raw materials that have been subjected to varying conditions of very high pressure and temperature. Some of the quartz used for electronics purposes also is manufactured in this way. There are, of course, other processes and numerous other synthetics, which may or may not match naturally occurring gemstones. As both the science and technology improve, more can be expected.

Synthetic gemstones offer a very serious challenge to those concerned with gem identification when chemical composition and crystal structure—the basic characteristics by which a gemstone is identified—are identical in both the manufactured product and its natural counterpart.

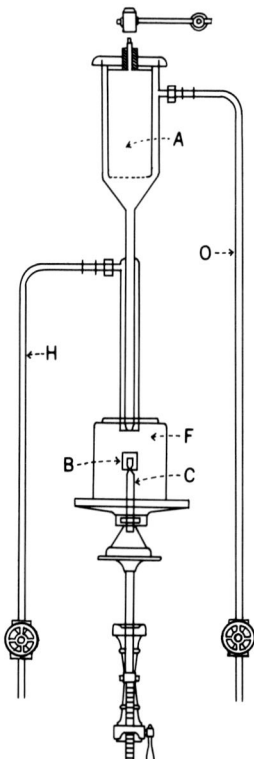

The Verneuil furnace, for making synthetic gem rough. A mixture of hydrogen (H) and oxygen (O) burns almost explosively, heating the fusion chamber (F) to high temperatures. Powdered aluminum oxide and appropriate coloring agents are sifted down from the hopper (A) to the fusion chamber and form a cylindrical boule (B) of ruby or sapphire on an adjustable stand (C).

V. GEM LORE

All sorts of magical and symbolic properties have been ascribed to gemstones through the ages; for example, the cat's-eye has been prescribed as a cure for paleness, citrine has been worn as a protection from danger, and the opal cherished as a symbol of hope. The result has been the creation of an intricate, chaotic, and contradictory but interesting mass of gem lore.

The Bible describes the jeweled breastplate worn by Aaron, first high priest of the Hebrews. After the destruction of the Temple and its restoration, a second breastplate was made and supposedly was modeled after the one worn by Aaron. As nearly as can be determined, in these plates were mounted twelve stones representing the Twelve Tribes of Israel. Among Christians, the Twelve Apostles also were represented symbolically by precious stones.

The Twelve Tribes	The Twelve Apostles
Levi, *Garnet*	Peter, *Jasper*
Zebulon, *Diamond*	Andrew, *Sapphire*
Gad, *Amethyst*	James, *Chalcedony*
Benjamin, *Jasper*	John, *Emerald*
Simeon, *Chrysolite*	Philip, *Sardonyx*
Issachar, *Sapphire*	Bartholomew, *Sard*
Naphtali, *Agate*	Matthew, *Chrysolite*
Joseph, *Onyx*	Thomas, *Beryl*
Reuben, *Sard*	James the Less, *Topaz*
Judah, *Emerald*	Jude, *Chrysoprase*
Dan, *Topaz*	Simon, *Hyacinth*
Asher, *Beryl*	Judas, *Amethyst*

The number "12" seems to follow a chain of gemstone superstitions. Gemstones were considered to have a mystical relationship not only with the Twelve Tribes and the Twelve Apostles, but also with the Twelve Angels, the Twelve Ranks of the Devil, and the Twelve Parts of the human body.

Some stones were even endowed with astrological significance and were believed to be in sympathy with the twelve zodiacal signs. On the basis of an elaborate system of prognostications, an astrologer was considered able to foretell future events by proper observance of changes in hue and brilliance of the symbolic stones.

Aries the Ram, *Bloodstone*	Libra the Scales, *Chrysolite*
Taurus the Bull, *Sapphire*	Scorpio the Scorpion, *Aquamarine*
Gemini the Twins, *Agate*	Sagittarius the Archer, *Topaz*
Cancer the Crab, *Emerald*	Capricornus the Goat, *Ruby*
Leo the Lion, *Onyx*	Aquarius the Water Bearer, *Garnet*
Virgo the Virgin, *Carnelian*	Pisces the Fishes, *Amethyst*

Perhaps in our own space-oriented times the ancient superstitions sympathetically relating certain gemstones with the planets will be revived. In the distant past, moonstone, topaz, and other white stones were believed to be in sympathy with the moon, diamond and ruby with the sun, jasper and emerald with Mars, amethyst, topaz, and emerald with Venus, carnelian, topaz, and amethyst with Jupiter, turquoise and sapphire with Saturn, and rock crystal, agate, and emerald with Mercury. Since Uranus, Neptune, and Pluto were unknown to the ancients, these planets have not been represented by gemstones.

Of special interest to the American public are birthstones. Many birthstone lists have been proposed, and in order to use this idea to popularize gemstones, the American jewelry industry has agreed upon an official list, which has served to bring about some uniformity in the selection of birthstones for the twelve months.

January, *Garnet*	July, *Ruby*
February, *Amethyst*	August, *Peridot* or *Sardonyx*
March, *Aquamarine* or *Bloodstone*	September, *Sapphire*
April, *Diamond*	October, *Opal* or *Tourmaline*
May, *Emerald*	November, *Topaz* or *Citrine*
June, *Moonstone* or *Pearl*	December, *Turquoise* or *Lapis lazuli*

All these associations and strange beliefs have served to create in the general public a mental image of gemstones that gives to them an increased exoticism and mysterious appeal far exceeding their monetary value.

VI. PRINCIPAL GEM SPECIES

An excursion into the literature of gems would reveal that there is much to be discovered about them other than the cold facts of gemology, techniques of gem cutting, and tales of gem lore. When all the information about an individual species is assembled, it provides a sketch of a fascinating gemstone personality. Whole books have been written about diamond—books filled with essays on its mining history, natural occurrences, scientific significance, and best-known cut stones.

In the following sections of this book, some of the facts about several of the better-known gem species have been gathered. The treatment is not meant to be complete, but enough information is given so that museum visitors may better understand and remember what they have seen.

For each species described there are color illustrations of certain gemstones displayed in the collection. Several photographic and artistic techniques have been used to emphasize the various aspects of the beauty of these stones, many of which are the largest and finest of their kinds known; however, not all of the finest gems are pictured here.

At the end of this descriptive section is a current list of the significant faceted gemstones in the collection. Obviously, this list will change, because new gemstones constantly are being acquired.

Diamond

Diamond is the king of gems. It is a form of pure carbon, and it is the hardest substance known; only diamond will cut diamond. It is interesting that the humble graphite, its close relative, is also pure carbon, but graphite is so soft and "slippery" that it is used as a lubricant and for making the "lead" in pencils.

The ancients believed diamond to be indestructible, and even today many people mistakenly believe that diamond cannot be broken. Despite its great hardness, however, diamond is not exceptionally tough, and it can be split along what diamond cutters call its *grain*.

The diamond's high brilliance results from its very high refraction, or ability to bend light, and its fire is caused by its high dispersion, or ability to divide light into its rainbow colors. However, only in properly cut stones are diamond's brilliance and fire developed to their maximum.

At great depths in the crust of the earth, and under conditions of very high pressure and temperature, diamonds form in pipelike bodies of kimberlite, a heavy, dark rock consisting primarily of two minerals, pyroxene and olivine. In South Africa diamonds are mined from the kimberlite, but they also are recovered there and elsewhere from beds of sand and gravel, where they have accumulated after being released from their mother rock by erosion.

Some of the world's largest diamond deposits are in Africa, and names such as Zaire, Sierra Leone, and the Union of South Africa bring to mind colorful legends of fabulous discoveries of diamond. Enormous deposits

The Hope diamond, because of its long and dramatic history and its rare deep-blue color, is probably the best known diamond in the world. By speculation, the Hope is linked to the famous "French Blue," which was brought to France from India in 1668 to become part of the crown jewels of King Louis XIV. The French Blue was stolen in 1792 and never recovered, but in 1830 an extraordinary 45½-carat blue diamond—presumably cut from the missing gem—came on the market. It was purchased by Henry Thomas Hope of England and became known by its present name. In 1949 the gem was acquired from the estate of Mrs. Evalyn Walsh McLean by Harry Winston, Inc., of New York. Ten years later this same company presented the gem, in Mrs. McLean's original setting, to the Smithsonian Institution.

The Eugenie Blue diamond, once the property of Empress Eugenie of France, is an extraordinary 31-carat, bright-blue, heart-shaped gem. It was presented to the Smithsonian Institution by Marjorie Merriweather Post.

Magnificent 12-carat "canary" diamond ring. Such pleasant and strongly colored diamonds are generally more valuable than colorless diamonds of equivalent size and quality.

This bright pink, pear-shaped, fancy-colored diamond from Tanzania, weighing 2.9 carats, was a gift to the collection from Sydney De Young. Diamonds of such intense pink color are extremely rare.

are also mined in Yakutia in Russia, mainly from along the Vilyui River. The output from this area makes Russia today the largest single producer of diamonds. Smaller deposits are found in South America—in Brazil, British Guiana, and Venezuela—and in India. Even in the United States some diamonds have been found—most coming from near Murfreesboro, Arkansas.

India was the most important source of diamond until 1728, when discoveries were made in Brazil. Among the important large diamonds found in India were the Koh-i-noor, the Great Mogul, and, very likely, the Hope diamond. Like India, Brazil in turn declined as a major source of diamond with the discovery and efficient recovery of large quantities in South Africa.

Diamonds are extremely rare even in diamond mines. For example, the famous South African mines contain only one part of diamond in more than 14 million parts of worthless rock. In spite of this, it is estimated that more than seven tons of gem- and industrial-quality diamond are mined around the world each year.

Among the British crown jewels is a cut diamond weighing 530.20 carats (more than 3¾ ounces), one of several stones that were cut from the largest gem diamond ever discovered. The rough stone, known as the Cullinan diamond, weighed 3,106 carats (almost 1¾ pounds) when it was found at the Premier Mine in South Africa in 1905. It appeared to have once been just part of a still larger stone.

Diamonds vary from colorless to black and from transparent to opaque. As they come from the mines, they are graded into two groups, gem and industrial. Those whose color, imperfection, or shape make them useless as gems—more than 8 out of every 10 carats mined—are used in industry. Diamonds of industrial quality also are produced synthetically, and these are used primarily in the manufacture of grinding wheels.

The best gem diamonds are flawless and are colorless or very slightly blue. Their value depends on their color, clarity, cut, and carat weight. Most costly are those called fancies, which have a distinct and strong color such as blue, pink, green, or deep yellow. Led by the Hope (blue), Victoria-Transvaal (champagne), Eugenie (blue), DeYoung (pink), and Shepherd (canary), the Smithsonian's collection is particularly rich in fancies.

Corundum: Includes Ruby and Sapphire

Both *ruby* and *sapphire,* which are second only to diamond in hardness among the gems, are of the mineral species corundum, an oxide of aluminum. They are identical in all characteristics except color. Most corundum is opaque, and it is mined in large quantities for use as an abrasive. In a few places, such as Moguk in Upper Burma and in Sri Lanka, clear corundum is found that is suitable for use as gems.

Red corundum is known as ruby. Its color, caused by traces of chromium, ranges from rose through carmine to a dark, slightly purplish red, referred to as pigeon's blood red. Rubies of this very desirable latter color often are called Burma rubies, and they are the most costly of all the corundum gems.

All gem corundum having a color other than red is sapphire. The name sapphire means blue, and this is the color most frequently associated with this gemstone. The finest sapphires are a velvety cornflower blue, and they come from Kashmir. Blue, white, yellow, gold, pink, and all the other colors of corundum are caused by the presence of slight traces of iron, chromium, titanium, and other metals present as dissolved impurities in the aluminum oxide. Frequently, sapphires are found that show patches of blue and yellow, or that have alternating zones of red and blue. Pure corundum is colorless.

Most gem corundum comes from the Orient, from localities such as Moguk in Upper Burma, near Bangkok in Thailand, Kashmir in India, and Sri Lanka. Because of this primarily Asian origin, the word oriental often is used with the names of other gems to denote a sapphire of a particular color. For example, green sapphire sometimes is called oriental emerald, and yellow sapphire sometimes is called oriental topaz.

There are some notable exceptions to the generally oriental occurrence of corundum. A little good-quality ruby has been found in North Carolina, and sapphire of high quality and many colors has come from Montana.

During the formation of a corundum crystal, extremely small, needlelike inclusions of rutile sometimes occur in it arranged according to the hexagonal pattern of the host crystal. When such inclusions are arranged in this way by nature, they cause, in properly cut stones, internal reflections that produce the optical phenomenon known as asterism. The effect is that of a six-rayed star, and the gems in which asterism occurs are known as star sapphires and star rubies. Asterism is rarer in ruby than in sapphire.

Since corundum is easily manufactured, synthetic ruby and sapphire are made and used extensively in jewelry. The synthetic stones can be distinguished from natural stones by microscopic examination of the kinds of inclusions and internal defects.

VARIETIES

Ruby: Red
Sapphire: Blue, yellow, pink, green, colorless, and any color except red

Star sapphire: Colored as sapphire and showing asterism
Star ruby: Red and showing asterism

Beryl: Includes Emerald and Aquamarine

Beryl is one of the most widely used colored gemstones, and under its several names in the gem world it is among the best known. When it is a rich green it is known as *emerald,* and when it is the blue green of sea water it is called *aquamarine.* Gem varieties such as the rose-pink *morganite,* golden-yellow *heliodor,* and colorless *goshenite* are less well known than emerald and aquamarine, but are equally attractive and satisfactory gemstones. Morganite in recent years has increased considerably in popularity.

Beryl is beryllium aluminum silicate. It frequently occurs in well-formed hexagonal crystals, and its many colors result from the presence of very small percentages of several different elements. Emerald owes its rich green color to traces of chromium, and the detection of the presence of this element is one of the means of identifying true emerald. Aquamarine, comprising the green and blue-green beryls, gets its color mainly from traces of iron. Practically all of the deep blue aquamarine available in jewelry stores results from the heat treating of greenish beryl or certain yellow-brown beryls. The stones are heated carefully to about 800° F., and the color change is permanent. The element lithium accounts for the color of pink beryl. As with aquamarine, the color of yellow beryl is now considered to be the result of traces of iron rather than uranium, as previously thought. Pure beryl is colorless.

A gift of Rosser Reeves, this extraordinary 138.7-carat star ruby may very well be the finest of its kind. The strong asterism, superb red color, unusual clarity, and large size for a ruby make this gem one of the most important in the entire collection.

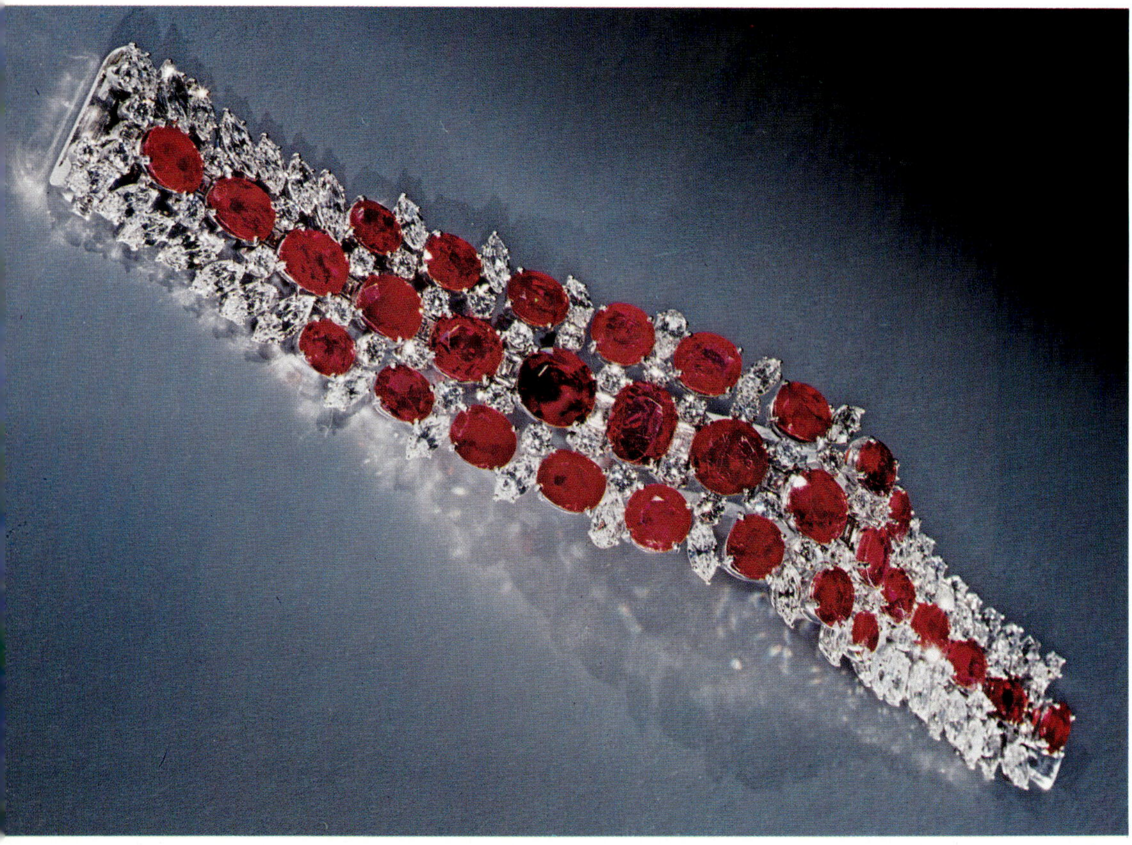

A king's ransom of thirty-one Burmese rubies of excellent color is set with eighty-six diamonds in a bracelet. The rubies exhibit very old cuts, but were purposely preserved that way by the owner when they were reset in the bracelet in 1951.

A suite of fine sapphires in some of the gem's more subtle colors. All from Sri Lanka, they weigh, from left to right, 42 carats, 20 carats, 31 carats, and 93 carats.

The 423-carat Logan sapphire, given by Mrs. John A. Logan, is a dazzling Sri Lanka gem set with twenty diamonds. It is most likely the largest gem sapphire of this coveted rich blue color known.

Beryl usually is found in pegmatites, which are very coarse-grained granite rocks formed by the cooling of molten material far beneath the earth's surface. As the rock cools and beryl and other crystals are formed, the stresses introduced are so great that the crystals frequently shatter so badly that they are useless as gem material. Frequently, too, impurities are introduced during crystal formation, and consequently the gem materials are found only where the crystals were able to form without interference—such as in openings or cavities in the rock.

Tremendous beryl crystals weighing as much as several tons each, but not of gem quality, have been discovered in a few localities. Large crystals of gem quality also occur in nature, and large cut stones of aquamarine and other colors of beryl are relatively common. Among the fine examples of beryl in the National Gem Collection is a remarkably large (2,054-carat), flawless cut stone of rich yellow green. This gem and others in the collection weighing 1,363 carats, 1,000 carats, 914 carats, 911 carats, and 578 carats accentuate the occurrence of large gem crystals of beryl in Brazil.

Fine emeralds are not found in pegmatites. At Muzo and elsewhere in Colombia, the most prolific source of the finest emeralds, they occur in veins with calcite, quartz, dolomite, and pyrite. The veins cut through dark-colored, carbonaceous limestone and shale. Large-scale mining at Muzo began 350 years ago and still continues sporadically to meet market requirements. Russian emeralds occur as good-sized crystals in mica schist, a metamorphic rock. They occur there with chrysoberyl, phenakite, and common beryl. Some of the smaller stones have good color and have been cut into valuable gems. Brazil, which produces many extraordinary aquamarines and other beryls, has not produced much quality emerald. Periodically, over the centuries, there have been reports of new discoveries of emerald, but so far none of these has begun to rival the Colombian source in either quantity or quality of the gems produced.

Although Brazil supplies the finest aquamarine and Colombia the finest emerald, several areas in the United States are sources of good-quality beryl of these colors. Foremost among these localities are Maine, California, and Connecticut for aquamarine and North Carolina for emerald. Morganite of pale pink to deep peach color, from California, is also notable. Various New England mines in Maine, New Hampshire, and Connecticut, and the gem mines of the Pala and Mesa Grande districts of California, have produced other colors of gem beryl. However, most of the beryl that has been mined in the United States has been used as an ore for beryllium, since little of it is of gem quality.

Because of its hardness (about 8), vitreous luster, beautiful color, and rarity, emerald always has been highly prized as a gem. Fine-quality emeralds may be as costly as fine diamonds. Other kinds of beryl have the same physical properties as emerald, but since they are less rare and less popular their relative value is lower.

Synthetic emerald of high gem quality has been marketed successfully. A synthetic substitute for aquamarine is also available; it is really a synthetic blue spinel. Certain other synthetics and blue topaz may also closely resemble aquamarine.

VARIETIES

Emerald: Grass green
Aquamarine: Blue green
Morganite: Pink

Heliodor: Yellow
Goshenite: Colorless

Pearl

The pearl is included among gemstones only because it is a beautiful object used in jewelry. As has been noted earlier, pearl is not technically a mineral because it is formed by the action of living organisms. However, the pearl has long occupied an important position among jewels, and it is unique in requiring little if any lapidary art to enhance its beauty. Nature has perfected pearls.

The ancient Chinese believed that pearls originated in the brain of a dragon. We now know, of course, that pearl is created by a secretion of a mollusk. Very few mollusks have the ability to produce the fine mother-of-pearl used in the jewelry trade, and even among those that can, very few produce pearls with iridescence, or *orient,* as it is known in the trade. Only two genera, the pearl oyster *(Margaritifera)* and the pearl mussel *(Unio),* are important sources of the gems. Edible oysters rarely produce pearls, and when they do, the pearls are of poor quality. Clams, of course, can also produce pearls, but they too are of generally poor quality.

The shells of pearl-producing mollusks are composed of layers of calcium carbonate in the form of either calcite or aragonite. These layers, cemented together with an organic substance known as conchiolin, are known as nacre. The layer closest to the animal is deposited in tiny, overlapping patches, producing an iridescent effect caused by the scattering of light rays reflected from the plates making up the nacre. The same material coats the surface of a gem pearl.

Seldom does a mollusk live out its time without attack by creatures boring through its shell, and without intrusion through the normal shell opening of tiny parasitic worms, sand, or other irritants. Usually, inert particles are forced by the animal against the inside of the shell, where they are covered with layers of pearl that fasten them to the shell. This is the source of most *blister pearls.* When the irritant remains in its fleshy part, the mollusk deposits a protective shell of pearl to cover it completely, and a spherical pearl may result. Pearls of less-symmetrical shape, called *baroques,* are more common.

The value of a pearl depends on its shape, color, orient, and size. Pearls of highest value are large, white with a faint tinge of pink or yellow, possess fine orient, are round, and are free of surface blemishes. The grading of pearls for color requires considerable experience to detect delicate differences. Various classification names, such as "rosée" for delicate pink shades, are used. Fancy colored pearls are those with a strong yellow, bronze, pink, green, blue, or black color. Grading for shapes, which differ markedly, is easier. Spherical pearls are usually drilled for beads; pear-shaped, or drop, pearls are used in earrings and pendants; and "boutons," or button-shaped pearls, with one flat side, are used for ear ornaments, cuff links, and rings. Irregular, baroque pearls and tiny seed pearls are used in jewelry designs, sometimes with noble metals and perhaps other gemstones.

The world's finest pearls, called *oriental pearls,* come from the fisheries of the Persian Gulf. Fine pearls also are found off the coasts of Burma, Tahiti, New Guinea, Borneo, Venezuela, and western South America, and in the Gulf of California. Fresh-water pearls of high quality, formed in pearl mussels, are found in various rivers in Europe and the United States, especially in rivers in the Mississippi Valley.

A method of growing *cultured pearls* has been well developed in Japan. A mother-of-pearl bead is inserted in the oyster as an irritant, and the animal is replaced in the sea in a cage. When oysters so treated are recovered after a period of three to seven years, the beads in the harvested

A recent gift of Janet Annenberg Hooker, this large, 75-carat square-cut Colombian emerald is remarkably free from internal flaws, which is an unusual condition for large emeralds.

Aquamarine is the gem name for a blue to blue-green variety of beryl. This 911-carat gem from Minas Gerais, Brazil, is not only a fine example for the color but is probably the largest gem aquamarine known.

Two large beryl gems of other colors. The rectangular pinkish morganite variety gem from Brazil, a gift of Mr. and Mrs. Frank Ix, weighs 236 carats and the pointed oval, green-gold gem from Madagascar weighs 134 carats.

Baroque or odd-shaped pearls, such as this lustrous trio of cultured pearls from Japan, are used in the preparation of interesting jewelry pieces. The ring contains a large, superb, natural pearl of black color from off the coast of Baja California.

crop usually are found to be coated with a layer of nacre up to almost a sixteenth of an inch thick.

The cultured pearl can be identified only by the observance—through a drill-hole or by X-ray—of the mother-of-pearl core, which had been inserted in the oyster. An instrument called an endoscope, devised for rapid testing of drilled pearls, relies on a beam of strong light carried by a hollow needle. The needle is inserted into the drill hole of the bead, and as it passes through the center portion of a natural pearl a flash of light, reflected through a mirror system in the needle, is observed. If no flash is observed it is a cultured pearl.

Topaz

Because shades of yellow are the most popular colors of topaz, it has become customary to believe that all topaz is yellowish. Also, there is a tendency to believe that all yellowish gemstones are topaz. Neither belief is correct. Stones of yellow, sherry, blue, pink, and colorless topaz all make beautiful gems, and their characteristics are identical except for color. On the other hand, citrine (a yellowish quartz), although entirely unrelated to topaz, often is disguised in the trade under the names Brazilian topaz, topaz quartz, or just topaz. Great numbers of stones described and sold as smoky topaz really are the much commoner citrine, which has few of the characteristics of fine topaz.

Topaz, an aluminum fluosilicate, has a hardness of 8, a vitreous luster, and a relatively high refractive index. It is found in near-perfect crystals that range in size from very small to very large, with some giants weighing as much as several hundred pounds. Most of these crystals, especially the largest ones, are colorless, a characteristic that indicates relatively high purity of composition. Although topaz gems have little fire, they take a high polish and can be very brilliant. Great care must be taken in cutting and polishing topaz because of its ready cleavage. The desired cut and high polish can be secured by avoiding excessive heat or pressure during the operation, and by planning facets so that none lies exactly parallel to the cleavage direction.

Although crystals of gem-quality topaz are found in many localities, perhaps the splendid blue ones from Russia and the yellow, wine, blue, and colorless ones from Brazil are best known. Some fine topaz has been found in the United States in such widely separated areas as New Hampshire, Texas, Colorado, and California. The light, golden-brown topaz from Colorado has an unfortunate tendency to fade in strong sunlight. It remains to be seen whether similar topaz coming from comparable occurrences in Mexico also will fade. By a system of heating and cooling, certain of the red-brown topaz crystals from Ouro Preto, Brazil, can be converted to colors ranging from salmon pink to purple red. Quick heating to high temperatures can completely remove color, and sudden or uneven cooling may cloud or crack the stone. A newer process can give certain colorless topaz a beautiful and permanent blue color through appropriate irradiation.

Opal

Opal has been admired for its great beauty since ancient times, but this gemstone lacked strong commercial appeal until the discovery of the Australian black opal late in the nineteenth century.

Opal is somewhat brittle, is sensitive to heat, and, in some cases, tends to deteriorate despite the best of care. Therefore, this stone lacks many of the physical characteristics required for an ideal gem. These deficiencies in durability would eliminate other species from the list of gemstones, but the great beauty of its flashing and shifting color patterns has made opal increasingly popular. Even its name, coming from the ancient Sanskrit "upala," means precious stone.

With a hardness between 5½ and 6½, opal is the softest of the more popular gems. It is just sufficiently hard, however, to be used in jewelry, where its setting usually helps to protect it from shock and abrasion.

Opal is unlike most gemstones in that its flashing color is not due to the color of the stone itself, or even to the color of its included impurities. Rather, it is due to the way in which tiny opal particles are grouped during its formation. Detailed photographs taken through an electron microscope show clearly how precious opal is deposited in nature as spheres so small that they are indistinguishable under powerful optical microscopes. These spheres are packed together in very orderly networks, row upon row and layer upon layer, with tiny open spaces, also in rows, between them. Masses of common opal lack this orderly internal arrangement of spheres. Since these rows of spheres in precious opal are spaced at distances approximately the same as the wavelength of light, a phenomenon known as *diffraction* occurs when white light hits the stone. The brilliant color flashes produced by diffraction are of different hues, depending on the sizes of the spheres of opal and, therefore, the distances between rows. To provide the best display of this optical effect, opal is almost always cut in cabochon form rather than as faceted stones.

Common opal, which shows milky opalescence, does not exhibit color flashes, and it is not often used as a gemstone. Each of the common varieties—such as hyalite, cacholong, and hydrophane—has its own slightly different set of characteristics, but only precious opal, with its dazzling color display, is important for gem purposes. To take full advantage of the small amounts of gem material available, or to bring out its color better, *precious* opal is often cut as thin pieces and mounted as doublets on some other backing. Also, the thin seams of precious opal in rock sometimes are cut so that the thin layer is exposed on a thicker backing of the adjoining rock. Precious opal, or gem opal, is classified as *white opal* when the color flashes are in a whitish or light background, *black opal* when the background material is gray, blue gray, or black, and *fire opal* when the background is more translucent and red, reddish orange, or reddish yellow.

Precious opal has been found in several areas of the world—in nodules, in seams in rock, or as replacements of other minerals or even of wood and shell. Hungarian deposits were well known in Roman times, but these and other deposits became insignificant with the discovery of opal in Australia in the late nineteenth century. Opal deposits were discovered in 1889 at White Cliffs in New South Wales, and other important discoveries in Australia followed, including deposits at Lightning Ridge in New South Wales that produce very dark stones and the rich fields of white opal at Coober Pedy in South Australia. Mexico has remained for a long time the principal source of richly colored fire opals, with the most important deposits located in the state of Querétaro, where mines have been worked intermittently since 1835. This has made the town of Querétaro today the center for the trade and cutting of Mexican opal. In more recent times fine quality gem opal has been appearing in considerable quantity from Brazil. Although great strides have been made in recent years in manufacturing opal substitutes and synthetics, gems from these classic occurrences are still highly treasured.

This rich sherry-colored oval gem of topaz weighing 129 carats is from Minas Gerais, Brazil.

A 3,273-carat topaz of soft blue natural color comes from Minas Gerais, Brazil. The Smithsonian Institution had this unique gem cut by John Sinkankas of California. For several years it was the largest topaz in the gem collection.

Fire opal, for which Mexico is famous, gets its name from the rich orange to red background color of the material, which may sometimes also display flashes of other colors. This superb fire opal from Jalisco, Mexico, weighs 30 carats and was cut by John Sinkankas.

A typical high-quality "black opal" weighing 27 carats from Lightning Ridge, Australia, given by Mrs. Oliver James. It is this kind of spectacular opal that has done most to create intense popular interest in all opal.

VARIETIES

White opal: Color flashes in light-colored background material
Black opal: Color flashes in dark gray or bluish background material

Fire opal: Orange or reddish background material

Spinel

Two of the more famous stones in the British crown jewels are the Black Prince's ruby and Timur ruby, but neither of these stones is really ruby. Like many gems long thought to be ruby, these two British stones are spinel. Although spinel occurs in many colors, such as yellow, green, violet, brown, and black, it is the red spinel that usually is seen in the gem trade. There are several names for varieties of red spinel, such as *ruby spinel, balas ruby, rubicelle,* and *almandine spinel*—all of which refer to the color resemblance to ruby.

Spinel is an oxide of magnesium and aluminum, and it is not closely related to ruby. However, because its hardness (8) is only somewhat less than that of ruby and its brilliance is about equal to that of ruby, spinel can make an excellent substitute for that gem. Also, because it is more plentiful, spinel costs much less. It is interesting that red spinel, like ruby, gets its color from the presence of traces of chromium.

Synthetic blue spinel is widely used as a substitute for aquamarine, and synthetic spinels of other colors are used as substitutes for many gems. However, the synthetic stones are not ordinarily made in the subtle shades so characteristic of natural spinel. Completely colorless spinel apparently exists only as a synthetic material. Actually, because of its hardness, durability, and many attractive colors, spinel makes a fine gemstone in its own right.

Like ruby and several other gemstones, spinel is found chiefly in the gem gravels of Sri Lanka, Burma, and Thailand. Appreciable amounts of spinel occur in the Sri Lanka gem gravels as worn, rounded pebbles of many colors. In the Burmese gravel deposits, the spinel is often found as well-formed octahedral crystals. Near Moguk, in Burma, spinel has been found in its original position in the limestone rocks as well as in the eroded stream deposits.

VARIETIES

Almandine spinel: Purplish red
Rubicelle: Orange red
Balas ruby: Rose red
Ruby spinel: Deep red
Chlorospinel: Translucent grass green

Ceylonite or pleonaste: Opaque dark green, brown, or black
Picotite or chrome spinel: Translucent dark yellow brown or green brown

Quartz: Includes Rock Crystal, Amethyst, and Citrine

Few gemstones can compete with quartz for variety of color. Having a hardness of 7, and occurring in many beautiful varieties, quartz is prevented from attaining a higher rank among gemstones only by its relative abundance.

The two kinds of quartz, crystalline and cryptocrystalline (fine-grained), occur in all kinds of mineral deposits throughout the world. Much of this material is suitable for gem cutting.

Colorless crystalline quartz, or *rock crystal,* makes attractive faceted gems, and it is used as a possible substitute for diamond and zircon, even though it lacks the fire and brilliance of those gemstones. Some very large, flawless crystals of colorless crystalline quartz have been found. The great Warner Crystal Ball, with a diameter of 12⅞ inches and weighing 106¾ pounds, was cut from such a crystal. Another unusual gem in the quartz collection is the 7,000-carat faceted quartz egg. In addition to the name rock crystal, colorless crystalline quartz sometimes appears in the jewelry trade under such names as rhinestone (not to be confused with the glass substitute), Herkimer diamond (from Herkimer County, New York), and Cape May diamond (from Cape May, New Jersey).

The most popular variety of quartz is *amethyst,* a transparent form whose color ranges from pale violet to deep purple. In many cut stones of amethyst the color intensity changes sharply from section to section. This is due to irregular color zoning common to amethyst crystals. The actual cause of the purple color amethyst is not very well understood. There are fewer cut stones of amethyst in very large sizes because of the rarity of large, flawless, well-colored crystals.

The name *citrine* (from the French word for lemon) attempts to describe the yellow color of another variety of quartz. Actually, the normal coloring of citrine varies from yellow to red orange and red brown, but the yellow sometimes rivals the yellow of topaz. In addition to the normal color range, the colors of citrine may grade through a grayish yellow variety known as *cairngorm* and a grayish variety called *smoky quartz* to a black variety called morion. Other varieties that add color dimensions to the group of quartz gemstones are *rose quartz* and *milky quartz*. As with amethyst, the reason for the color in rose quartz has not been definitely established. Milky quartz owes its color to myriads of tiny cavities containing fluids.

The range of colors in quartz is somewhat surprising, considering that the mineral is a simple silicon dioxide. Some of the colors, as with corundum and some other gemstones, are due to traces of impurities. In quartz, these impurities consist mainly of oxides of iron, manganese, and titanium. However, as already suggested, all the reasons for quartz coloration in its many varieties are not known.

In addition to possessing wide variation of color, quartz, like sapphire and certain other gemstones, can exhibit asterism or chatoyancy. The well-known *tiger's-eye* from West Griqualand, South Africa, owes its eye effect to the fact that its material is a replacement of fibrous asbestos by cryptocrystalline quartz. The color of tiger's-eye arises from the partial alteration of the asbestos to yellow-brown iron oxides before it is replaced by quartz. Inclusions of rutile, tourmaline, or actinolite needles may produce attractive patterns in quartz, but they do not always cause chatoyancy. The material containing such inclusions is called sagenitic quartz, or it may be descriptively named, such as rutilated quartz, tourmalinated quartz, and so forth. Sagenitic quartz is usually cut as cabochons rather than as faceted stones since the inclusions are of greater interest than the quartz itself.

If the foreign inclusions consist of tiny flakes of hematite or mica, the quartz assumes a spangled appearance and is called *aventurine.*

Crystals of quartz varieties that are opaque or that contain visible inclusions normally are cut as cabochons to take advantage of the body color or to make the inclusions more visible. Crystals of the transparent varieties are fashioned in any of several cutting styles, depending on whether it is

From left, a rosy pink 22-carat gem, one of ruby red weighing 36 carats, and a steely blue 30-carat gem illustrate the broad range of attractive colors found in spinel. The center gem is from Burma, the others are from Sri Lanka.

A wide range of quartz colors is seen here in gems selected from the collection. They include, from left, a 90-carat smoky quartz from Switzerland, a 358-carat colorless rock crystal from Brazil, a 61-carat amethyst from Brazil, a 278-carat citrine from Brazil, and an 84-carat rose quartz from Brazil. The citrine and rose quartz were cut and donated by A. R. Cutter.

This modern-day snuff bottle of Australian chrysoprase—a green variety of quartz—with a ruby crystal stopper was carved by Mrs. Helen Hanke.

desired to take maximum advantage of color or of brilliance. Because of its availability in fairly large, flawless pieces in various colors, quartz has been used extensively in carving. The Chinese have excelled in carving large, ornate objects of rock crystal and the master carvers of Idar-Oberstein in West Germany are noted for the quality and versatility of their carvings in all sorts of quartz materials.

Although quartz occurs in many varieties and its crystals are cut in many styles, it is easily identified by its refractive index of 1.55, specific gravity of 2.65, and hardness of 7.

CRYSTALLINE VARIETIES

Amethyst: Purple to violet
Cairngorm: Smoky yellow
Citrine: Yellow to red orange and red brown
Milky quartz: White
Morion: Black
Rock crystal: Colorless
Rose quartz: Rose to pink
Smoky quartz: Gray to black

CRYPTOCRYSTALLINE VARIETIES (CHALCEDONY)

Agate: Pronounced color banding
Aventurine: Inclusions of sparkling flakes
Bloodstone: Dark green dotted with red
Carnelian: Red to yellow red
Cat's-eye: Chatoyant
Chrysoprase: Green
Jasper: Opaque brown to red brown, green, yellow, etc.
Onyx: Color banding in straight layers of contrasting color
Sard: Light to dark brown
Sardonyx: Sard or carnelian bands alternating with white bands
Tiger's-eye: Bright brownish yellow, sometimes blue; chatoyant

Chrysoberyl: Includes Alexandrite and Cat's-eye

With color ranging from shades of yellow and brown through blue green to olive, and with a hardness of 8½, chrysoberyl has most of the characteristics necessary for a fine gem. Rare stones of high-quality chrysoberyl demand high prices, and they are sought eagerly by the connoisseur of gemstones.

Chrysoberyl is beryllium aluminate, and thus is chemically related to the gemstone spinel, which is magnesium aluminate. When pure, chrysoberyl is colorless and relatively uninteresting as a gemstone because of its lack of color dispersion and its moderate refractive index of 1.75. However, few pure samples are known, as chrysoberyl normally contains some iron or chromium in place of aluminum and some iron in place of beryllium. As a result of such impurities, the color of chrysoberyl may be yellowish, green, or brownish.

Chrysoberyl and beryl are the only important gemstones containing the element beryllium. The minerals beryllonite, euclase, hambergite, and phenakite also contain this element, but they are rare and seldom are seen as cut gems.

The *alexandrite* variety of chrysoberyl has two colors in delicate balance, and it changes from a columbine red to an emerald green when viewed under different light. When viewed in daylight, which is richer in green, the color balance shifts toward green, and that hue is seen by the observer. Under artificial light, normally richer in red, the color balance shifts toward red, and the stone seems to have changed to that color. This extremely rare stone, named after Czar Alexander II of Russia, because it was discovered on his birthday in 1830, is found only occasionally, primarily in Russia, Sri Lanka, Rhodesia, and Brazil. The Russian stones, found with emerald in mica schist, tend to be smaller than the Sri Lanka stones and have a color change going from emerald green to violet red. Found as pebbles in gem gravels, the Sri Lanka stones have a color change going from a less-emerald green to a browner red. The 66-carat, record-size alexandrite in the National Collection shows the color change typical of Sri Lanka stones. Quality Rhodesian stones have a good red phase, but tend to be smaller. Brazilian alexandrites, a much more recent introduction to the gem market, are of good size with excellent color change and some even show a typical chrysoberyl cat's-eye in addition. A synthetic stone is commonly marketed as alexandrite, but this substitute not only is man-made but is actually synthetic corundum instead of synthetic chrysoberyl.

Cat's-eye chrysoberyl contains myriads of tiny fiberlike channels arranged in parallel position. When the stone is cut as a cabochon, a band of light is reflected from the curved top of the stone, producing an effect that resembles the split pupil of a cat's-eye. Certain large cat's-eye chrysoberyl gems from Sri Lanka deserve to be classed among the most beautiful gems of the world.

VARIETIES

Alexandrite: Green in daylight, changing to red in artificial light

Cat's-eye: Chatoyant

Tourmaline

The name *tourmaline,* like the name *garnet,* is actually the name given to a family consisting of several very closely related mineral species. Most gem tourmalines should correctly carry their species names of *elbaite* or *liddicoatite.* Because of its great color range, which includes pink, green, blue, yellow, brown, and black in many different shades and combinations of shades, tourmaline is one of the most popular of the colored gemstones. Tourmaline with a color near emerald green is particularly popular, and reddish shades are now beginning to capture public fancy.

Chemically, all tourmalines are very complex borosilicates, and their color is determined by the various elements present. Tourmaline crystals having sodium, lithium, or potassium are either colorless, red, or green; those having iron are blue, blue green, or black; and those having magnesium are colorless, yellow brown, or blackish brown.

Some crystals of tourmaline are of two or more colors, and stones of mixed colors, such as pink and green, can be cut from these. The color mixing may show as zoning with the core color of the crystal overlaid by another color and perhaps with even additional layers of other colors. Zoned crystals with a core of deep pink covered by a layer of green have been called "watermelon tourmaline." Because its refractive index of about 1.6 is too low to give it marked brilliance, and its color dispersion is too low to give it fire, the tourmaline relies almost solely on the beauty of its color for its rank in popularity.

Although tourmaline has a low refractive index and low dispersion, it exhibits remarkable dichroism. In other words, it can present different tints to the viewer depending on the direction that the light is traveling through the crystal. When viewed down the long or vertical axis of the crystal, the

One of the finest quality chrysoberyl cat's eyes in existence is the 58-carat Maharani from Sri Lanka.

Shown here in its reddish phase under incandescent lighting, this superb gem of the alexandrite variety of chrysoberyl also has a fine greenish color in daylight. The 10-carat gem from Sri Lanka was a gift of Mrs. George H. Johnson.

In addition to its fine cat's-eyes and its color-changing alexandrite varieties, chrysoberyl occurs in handsome stones that vary considerably in color. This 114-carat gem from Minas Gerais, Brazil, is typical.

Green seems to be the best known color of commercial tourmaline, but this extremely variable gem family exhibits many subtle color blends, such as those shown here. At left is a 110-carat stone, at upper center a 173-carat stone, at lower center a 40-carat stone, and at right a 62-carat stone. All are from Brazil except the largest, which comes from Mozambique.

color of tourmaline is much stronger than when viewed from the side. This means that if the original crystal is dark the cutter will have to cut the stone with the flat part, or table, parallel to the long axis of the crystal. The color of the gemstone then will be lightened when viewed from its table, since this is the direction of lighter color. Similarly, the table of a lighter-colored crystal can be cut perpendicular to the long axis in order to produce a deeper-colored gem.

Some tourmaline crystals contain threadlike tubes of inclusions of microscopic size running parallel to the length. When cut as cabochons, such crystals give a good "cat's-eye" effect.

Tourmaline has no distinct cleavage and has a hardness somewhat above 7, and these characteristics make the stone sufficiently resistant to normal shock and wear so that it is highly satisfactory for use in jewelry.

Noted deposits of tourmaline are located in the Ural Mountains of Russia, Sri Lanka, Burma, Southwest Africa, Madagascar, Brazil, Maine, and California. Crystals from each of these localities seem to have their own color specialties. The deposits in San Diego County, California, are unique in that all colors except brown are found there. In the early 1900s pink and red tourmaline was shipped from there to China for carving, but this thriving trade stopped with the end of Chinese imperial reign. Gems mined in this area now go directly into world-wide commerce with the bulk of production coming from the Stewart Mine of Pala Properties International. The tourmaline deposits at Paris, Auburn, Hebron, and elsewhere in Maine, have furnished a number of excellent gems, especially of blue and green colors. Recent discoveries at the properties of Plumbago Mining Company in Maine have brought new life to this tourmaline source. These two deposits are the primary source of quality commercial gems from the United States at this time.

VARIETIES

Achroite: Colorless
Indicolite: Blue

Dravite: Brown
Schorl: Black
Rubellite: Pink

Zircon

Zircon, because of its very high refractive index and high dispersion, approaches diamond in degree of brilliance and fire. On only casual examination it is quite possible to mistake a well-cut, colorless zircon for a diamond. However, a careful examination of the back facets of such a stone, when viewed through the table, would show strong double refraction, a characteristic of zircon but not of diamond. Zircon's double refraction makes the back facet edges appear doubled. Since diamond is "singly refracting," it cannot produce this double appearance of the back facets.

Zircon is brittle and has a hardness of just over 7, while diamond's hardness, as we have seen, is rated at 10. After being worn in jewelry for a long period of time, zircon will show signs of chipping on the facet edges. Under the same conditions, diamond would remain unchanged. Because of this tendency for facet edges to chip, it is the practice in the gem trade to pack cut zircons separately. If a number of zircons were placed in the same paper packet there would be a risk of "paper wear."

In the gem trade, the most important zircons are those that are colorless, golden brown, or sky blue. Such stones originally were reddish-brown zircon pebbles from Indochina, but they have been converted by being subjected to temperatures approaching 1,800° F. for periods of up to two hours. When the original zircons are heated in a closed container, the stones become blue or colorless; when a flow of air is allowed through the container, the stones become golden yellow, red, or colorless. In most of these converted stones the color remains quite stable, but in some it may revert to an unattractive greenish or brownish blue after a period of time.

In addition to being reddish brown, natural zircon may vary from almost colorless to yellow, red, orange, and brown or from yellow green to dark green and, occasionally, blue. Green stones occur when the material has been subjected to natural radioactivity in its original deposit.

The most important producing areas of gem zircon are in a region of Indochina that comprises parts of Thailand, Vietnam, and Laos. Additional gem zircon, like so many of the other gem species, is recovered from near Moguk in Upper Burma and from the gem gravels of Sri Lanka.

There is no synthetic zircon on the market, but a bright blue synthetic spinel is sometimes used to simulate zircon successfully. Because of the introduction of so many new and suitable synthetic gem materials, zircon is seldom used as a diamond substitute in modern jewelry.

Peridot

The relative rarity of peridot and the ease with which it can be simulated in glass, whose luster it approximates, probably account in good part for the low popular demand for this gemstone. Although peridot has little brilliance and no fire, its unusual color and glassy luster produce a unique effect that serves to make it attractive.

The color of peridot is an unusual bottle green that shades, in some stones, toward yellow green and, more rarely, toward brown. In 1952 it was discovered that almost all of the brown gems believed to have been peridot in various gem collections were actually of an entirely unrelated species, which since has been named sinhalite. Brown peridot still remains rare and is somewhat of a collector's item.

The green of peridot, which is quite different from the green of other gemstones, is due to some iron included in its composition. It is suspected that a trace of nickel contributes to the liveliness of the color.

Peridot has a hardness of only 6½ and a rather strong tendency to cleave, and these characteristics reduce its value for use in jewelry exposed to rough wear. It is more safely used in pins, earrings, and pendants that in rings.

Peridot is a gem name for the common mineral olivine, an iron magnesium silicate. Olivine is found in numerous places, and small, gemmy pieces are found in many localities. Many of the largest and best gems of peridot have come from mines on the Egyptian island of Zebirget (Island of St. John) in the Red Sea, but most gem peridot now comes from Burma and elsewhere. Great numbers of smaller stones have been cut from olivine found in Arizona gravels.

Centuries ago, peridot was known by the name topaz, since the stones came from Topazos, the island now known as Zebirget (Zeberged). The name topaz, as we have seen, is used today for an entirely different mineral species.

Spodumene

Spodumene, a lithium aluminum silicate, is one of the very few gemstones containing lithium. It has had more acceptance as a gemstone in the

The beautiful colors of these brilliant zircons are the result of artificial heat treatment given to natural, reddish-brown stream pebbles. Such treatment is common for aquamarine, tanzanite, and other gems. The four zircons here are, left to right, 103 carats from Indochina, 106 carats from Thailand, 48 carats and 98 carats from Sri Lanka.

An enormous 310-carat, fine-quality peridot from Zebirget, Egypt, is the largest on record, and came to the Smithsonian with the Roebling collection. It is flanked by a 9-carat peridot from Arizona at left and a 46-carat stone, also from Zebirget, at right.

Many of the larger and better-quality stones of spodumene, usually in shades of green and yellow green, come from Brazil. This square-cut 69-carat gem is a fine example.

Its 880-carat size makes this one of the largest gems of the kunzite variety of spodumene known. Remarkably, it is also practically flawless.

United States than elsewhere, a situation due to early discoveries of unique occurrences of a lavender-pink variety at Branchville, Connecticut, in 1879 and in San Diego County, California, about twenty years later. At the time of the discovery of the California material, the variety was named *kunzite* in honor of G. F. Kunz, a noted American gemologist of the time.

The finding of a bright green variety, *hiddenite,* in North Carolina about 1880 greatly stimulated the interest of American gem collectors. Some of the bright green spodumene coming from Brazil in recent years compares very favorably in color with North Carolina hiddenite. Unfortunately, hiddenite can be temporarily simulated by the artificial irradiation of other kinds of spodumene. Other than in a scattered few of these unusual occurrences of kunzite and hiddenite, spodumene usually is found in yellow and yellow-green shades, with Brazil, Madagascar, and Afghanistan being the chief sources.

Spodumene has a hardness of about 7, but with a refractive index of about 1.66 and a low dispersion there seems to be relatively little to recommend it as a gemstone. The fact that it exhibits a very strong tendency to cleave in two different directions would seem to rule it out completely as being too difficult to cut. Nevertheless, the production and purchase of cut stones of spodumene persist because of the beauty of the gem.

The kunzite and hiddenite varieties of spodumene show strong *pleochroism,* or the ability to show three different colors when viewed in the direction of different axes. Some of the large Brazilian kunzite crystals mined in the early 1960s have an intense rose-violet color when viewed along the long axis of the crystal, but have pale blue-violet and pale-tan to greenish colors when viewed from the other two directions. When heat-treated, or exposed to strong light, this Brazilian kunzite loses its tan and bluish colors but retains the intense rose violet. Because of spodumene's pleochroism, the direction of cutting in the stones becomes extremely important, as it must be done in a manner that will take advantage of the violet color in kunzite and the green color in hiddenite:

VARIETIES

Kunzite: lavender to magenta   *Hiddenite:* green

Garnet

The name garnet is applied to a group of at least six very closely related silicate minerals that are alike in crystal structure but that differ mainly in the substitution of certain metallic elements in their composition. These minerals are:

Pyrope, magnesium aluminum garnet
Almandine, iron aluminum garnet
Spessartine, manganese aluminum garnet
Uvarovite, calcium chromium garnet
Grossular, calcium aluminum garnet
Andradite, calcium iron garnet

Most natural garnets have compositions intermediate between members of the basic group of six. For example, there are garnets having compositions anywhere between pyrope and almandine, depending on the amount of difference in the magnesium or iron content. These same garnets may even have varying amounts of manganese, and thus be partially spessartine.

The six garnets in the basic group are found in considerable quantity in many areas, some of sufficiently high quality to be considered gemstone material. Even when stones of gem quality are found, their colors—

particularly the reds—tend to be so intense that they seem to be opaque. But in recent years bright, transparent garnets in greens, tans, browns, and other colors—and some even colorless—have reached the gem market in quantity.

Garnet has a hardness (about 7) suitable for gemstone material and a fairly high refractive index (1.74 and above).

Ruby red pyrope has been the most popular variety of garnet with tsavorite and demantoid the most valuable. Pyrope is found in Bohemia, Czechoslovakia, where it occurs as small, poorly shaped crystals. Red pyrope also is found in Africa, where it is called Cape ruby, and in Arizona, where it is sold as Arizona ruby. Another kind of pyrope called *rhodolite* is noted for its soft, rosy purple color. Actually, rhodolite is one of the intermixed garnets with a composition somewhere between pyrope and almandine. Many of the finest rhodolite gems have come from North Carolina and Zaire.

Almandine is popular in its deep red, transparent form, but since the red is so dark and intense that it appears black, the stones usually are cut as cabochons with the back hollowed out. This makes them thinner, and thus lightens their color. Garnets cut in this manner are all known as carbuncles. Brazil, India, Sri Lanka, Australia, and parts of the United States are important sources of almandine.

Although spessartine has a rich orange color, it is not often used as a gemstone because of the relative rarity of gem-quality cutting material. This mineral gets its name from the town of Spessart, Germany, where it was first found. Excellent spessartine with colors ranging from orange to brown has been found at Amelia Court House, Virginia, and quality gems have been cut from such material. Sri Lanka, Burma, Madagascar, and Brazil also have furnished fine gem spessartine.

The chromium garnet, uvarovite, is always too poor in quality for cutting. Uvarovite crystals, which are emerald green in color, usually occur in only small sizes and even then do not have the necessary transparency. They are found mostly in Russia, Finland, and California.

Grossular varies in color. It occurs chiefly in some shade of red, green, yellow, or brown, depending on the impurities present. When pure, grossular is colorless. A kind of grossular called *hessonite* has an attractive cinnamon color, and is found mainly in Sri Lanka. Because of its color it can easily be confused with spessartine, which it closely resembles. Supplies of a superb, almost emerald-green, vanadium-bearing grossular have been coming from Kenya and Zaire. It is in commerce under the trade name of tsavorite.

Andradite, a very common garnet, usually is found in shades of red, black, brown, yellow, or green. Some types of gem andradite have special names for different colors: *topazolite,* yellow; *demantoid,* green; and *melanite,* sparkling black. The very valuable demantoid comes primarily from Russia and Italy.

VARIETIES

Grossular: Colorless, green, amber, brownish yellow, rose
  Hessonite: Cinnamon colored
  Tsavorite: Bright green
Pyrope: Deep red
  Rhodolite: Rose red and purple
Almandine: Deep red
Spessartine: Brownish red to orange

Andradite: Yellow, greenish yellow, emerald green, brownish red, brownish yellow, brown, black
  Topazolite: Yellow to greenish
  Demantoid: Grass green to emerald green
  Melanite: Black
Uvarovite: Green

Garnets occur in many colors. The large, 74-carat rhodolite garnet at left from Tanzania, gift of John Saul, and the 109-carat spessartine garnet at right from Brazil are of the more traditional red color. The 9-carat orange grossular garnet is from Sri Lanka and the 10-carat green demantoid garnet is from Russia.

The Jade Dragon Vase, standing 14 inches tall, is carved of rare lavender "Imperial" jadeite jade in the Ch'ien Lung style. The carving is modern, of unknown origin, and a gift of Marjorie Merriweather Post.

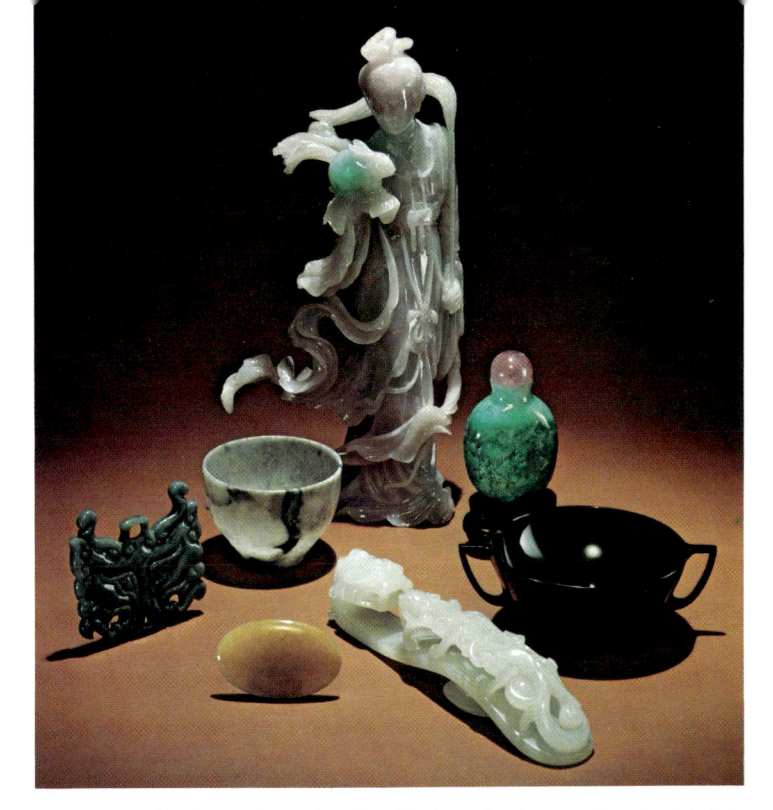

A selection of jade carvings of various kinds and colors cut from both jadeite and nephrite jade material found in Wyoming, California, Guatemala, and Burma.

A pair of altar lanterns from the Imperial collection of ritual vessels carved in nephrite jade for the Chinese Emperor Ch'ien Lung about A.D. 1750. Later they were in the private collections of Tsang Dan-Zu of Nanzing and of Maude Monell Vetlesen of New York.

Jade

The name jade is applied today to two unrelated minerals—*nephrite* and *jadeite*—that have somewhat similar characteristics.

Jadeite, the rarer of the two, is a sodium aluminum silicate that belongs to a group of rock-forming minerals known as pyroxenes. Its color varies from white to emerald green, magenta, and many other colors. Jadeite is highly prized, and when it occurs as emerald green it is considered one of the most valuable gemstones. This kind of jade is found in several places, but the most important occurrence is in Upper Burma. Nephrite, a more common species, is a calcium magnesium iron silicate belonging to a group of rock-forming minerals known as amphiboles. The color varies from white, bright green to a dark spinach green and black. Among the places where nephrite occurs are New Zealand, Turkestan, Siberia, Alaska, Taiwan, China, Silesia, and certain parts of the western United States, notably in Wyoming and California.

Jade is not particularly hard (6½), but it is very tough, and this characteristic makes it an excellent material for carving. Even when subjected to punishing usage, jade resists chipping and wear. It was used for making tools and weapons by primitive peoples who lived in what is now Mexico, Switzerland, France, Greece, Egypt, Asia Minor, and in other places. The jade implements fashioned by these peoples have survived well the ravages of time.

The Chinese and Japanese prize jade highly. In their countries, tradition has assigned to jade medicinal and spiritual values, and has associated with it the cardinal virtues of charity, modesty, courage, justice, and wisdom. As a consequence, these peoples long ago developed the carving of jade as a high art. Among the magnificent Chinese jade carvings in the National Gem Collection are 140 pieces produced mostly during the Ching Dynasty (1644-1912), when the art of jade carving was at its peak. Many of these jades were carved in imitation of the revered bronze ceremonial vessels of ancient times. This collection was presented to the Smithsonian Institution in 1959 by Edmund C. Monell in behalf of the estate of his mother, Mrs. Maude Monell Vetlesen of New York.

Gemstones for the Collector

A number of mineral species have produced cut gemstones that fulfill enough of the necessary requirements of beauty, durability, and rarity, but their popularity and commercial success have been sharply limited because of insufficient supply. In some cases of even adequate supply such gemstones do not compete with other, more plentiful kinds that exhibit the same characteristics. The scarcity of these minerals does not diminish their standing as potential gem material—it merely points up the effect of accidental natural distribution of these species.

Among the rarer minerals that produce good gemstones are cordierite, benitoite, euclase, phenakite, beryllonite, willemite, wernerite, danburite, datolite, axinite, brazilianite, andalusite, sillimanite, kyanite, kornerupine, enstatite, diopside, epidote, sphene, sinhalite, and orthoclase. Willemite, a rare zinc silicate found in only a few localities, is typical of these rarer minerals. The famous zinc mines at Franklin, New Jersey, produced a few large, gemmy crystals of willemite, and some fine gemstones were cut from some of these. Willemite's borderline hardness of 5 to 5½ and its extreme rarity effectively eliminate it from the gem market, but the collector who is able to obtain a good stone of this material is indeed fortunate.

Some mineral species, although beautiful when cut, and prized by collectors, are entirely too soft, too easily cleaved, or have some other physical weakness that renders them useless as commercial gemstones. Sphalerite, apatite, fluorite, calcite, cerussite, zincite, and hematite are included in this group. Sphalerite is typical; it produces brilliant and colorful gemstones that hold their own among other stones of great beauty. Unfortunately, this zinc sulfide, with a hardness of 3½ to 4, is so soft and cleaves so readily that it is very difficult to cut properly, and it cannot be used in jewelry.

Nevertheless, rare or not, soft or not, such gems as those described here are eagerly sought by gem collectors and are abundant in the Smithsonian collection.

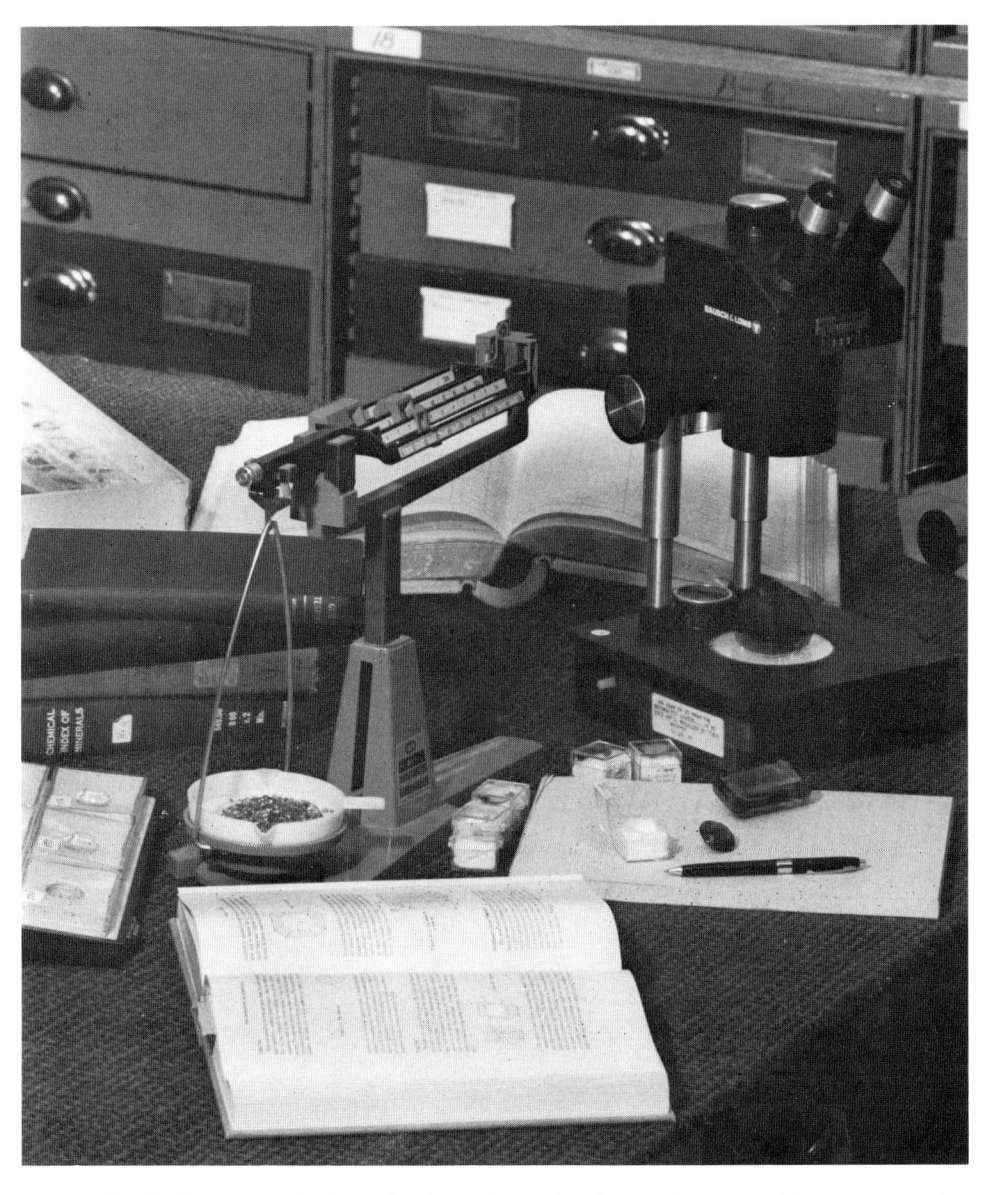

The Smithsonian maintains collections of gems for all sorts of purposes. The research and reference collections, unlike those for exhibition and education, are not usually available to the general public.

Exotic gems for the collector. The large, 288-carat scapolite is from Burma. From left, the others are a 27-carat phosphophyllite from Bolivia, gift of Dr. and Mrs. Korfmacher; an 8-carat benitoite from California; and a 30-carat labradorite from Idaho. All four gems are the largest of their kinds on record.

A rare gem of orthoclase feldspar from Madagascar. At 250 carats it is the largest on record.

This large gold chalice was made in St. Petersburg, Russia, in 1791 by order of Empress Catherine the Great as a memorial to General Potemkin. It is studded with intaglios and cameos of carnelian, bloodstone, and other ornamental materials, and embellished with 1,300 diamonds. Gift of Marjorie Merriweather Post.

A crown containing 950 Brazilian or Indian diamonds weighing 700 carats and 79 turquoise cabochons weighing 540 carats. When Napoleon I gave the crown to Empress Marie Louise in 1811, to celebrate the birth of their son, it contained emeralds rather than turquoise. Gift of Marjorie Merriweather Post.

VII. JEWELRY

It is often difficult to divorce the thought of gemstones from the idea of jewelry, for which most of them were originally intended. As might be expected, then, there are a number of important jewelry pieces in the National Collection of Gems—including the Hope diamond necklace itself. Any piece of jewelry that is included in the collection either contains major gems or has an exceptionally rich assemblage of them, because the historic, artistic, and esthetic aspects of jewelry are not a primary concern. Only the gems themselves have a legitimate claim to inclusion in a natural history collection.

Nevertheless, any rich assemblage of gems in a jewelry setting often guarantees that it will at least be dazzling and may very well have had a fascinating history. Thus, three of the four greatest diamonds in the collection—the Hope diamond and the Victoria-Transvaal diamond in necklaces, the Eugenie blue diamond in a ring—are mounted in jewelry. In their case, as is also true of the Logan sapphire, the Bismarck sapphire, and others, a single great gem dominates its setting, which merely serves to accentuate and support it. Other jewelry pieces, such as the Napoleon necklace and the Marie Antoinette earrings, contain important gems, but the primary impact comes from their fascinating histories and not from the gems. Still other beautiful jewelry pieces in the collection contain no highly significant gems but are studded with many of them, which tends to produce a luxurious effect. The Catherine the Great chalice with its 1,300 diamonds or the Empress Marie Louise tiara with its 950 diamonds are of this last sort. Preferably, the quality of the gems it contains, but sometimes the sheer quantity, tends to guarantee a place for a piece of jewelry in the collection. Thus, over a period of time, like the great crown jewel collections of the world, the Smithsonian's gem collection has acquired considerable jewelry fit for a queen.

CHARACTERISTICS OF SOME COMMON GEMS

Approximate average of

Species	hardness	specific gravity	refractive index	dispersion	durability	Usual color range
Beryl	7¾	2.70	1.58	Low	High	Green (emerald), blue green (aquamarine), pink (morganite), colorless (goshenite)
Chrysoberyl	8½	3.71	1.75	Low	High	Yellow, green, brown
Corundum	9	4.00	1.77	Low	High	Red (ruby), various (sapphire)

CHARACTERISTICS OF SOME COMMON GEMS (continued)

Approximate average of

Species	hardness	specific gravity	refractive index	dispersion	durability	Usual color range
Diamond	10	3.52	2.42	High	High	Colorless
Garnet group	7½	3.70–4.16	1.74–1.89	Medium to high	High	Yellow, red, green brown
Jade (nephrite)	6½	2.96	1.62	None	High	Green, white
Jade (jadeite)	7	3.33	1.66	None	High	Green, white
Opal	6	2.10	1.45	None	Low	Red, dark gray, orange, white, with or without vari-colored fire
Pearl	3½	2.71	None	None	Low	White
Peridot	6½	3.34	1.68	Low	Medium	Yellow green, brownish green
Quartz	7	2.65	1.55	Low	High	Purple (amethyst), yellow (citrine), colorless (rock crystal)
Spinel	8	3.60	1.72	Low	High	Shades of red, green, blue, violet
Spodumene	7	3.18	1.66	Low	Low	Colorless, pink, yellow, green
Topaz	8	3.54	1.63	Low	Medium	Colorless, sherry, pink, blue
Tourmaline	7	3.06	1.63	Low	High	Wide range, except bright red
Zircon	7	4.02	1.81	High	High	Almost colorless, blue, brown, green, yellow

VIII. GEMS IN THE COLLECTION

The Smithsonian's collection of gems continues to grow and improve constantly, and it changes character continually as important new gemstones are added and less important ones are retired. A sampling of significant gems currently in the collection is itemized in the following list. Included are some of the largest gems of each kind, some of the more interesting stones, and some small gems notable for the places from which they came. Though listed by species and size, some of the largest stones are not included because they are not particularly significant; neither are most cabochons, rough opal, beads, carvings, and spheres, even though these objects may be fine examples of their kinds.

The descriptions listed include, in order: weight in carats; color; popular name or other description, if any; place of origin; National Museum of Natural History catalog number; and name of donor.

DIAMOND

127	colorless (the Portuguese), Brazil, 3898
67.9	champagne (the Victoria-Transvaal), South Africa, 7101, Wilkinson
45.5	blue (the Hope), India, 3551, Winston
36	colorless (Marie Antoinette earring), unknown, 5018-1, Barzin
36	colorless (Marie Antoinette earring), unknown, 5018-2, Barzin
31	blue (the Eugenie Blue), South Africa, 4873, Post
29.3	colorless, South Africa, 4220, Riggs
22	pale yellow, South Africa, 7107, Wilkinson
18.3	yellow (the Shephard), South Africa, 3406
16.7	colorless, South Africa, 7114 Pearson
12	yellow, South Africa, 4668, James
9	black, South Africa, 8043, Roebling
7.9	colorless (the Humphrey), unknown, 5274
3.4	green (irradiated), unknown, 7105, Wilkinson
2.9	pink, Tanzania, 3772, De Young
2.3	colorless, Arkansas, 8050, Lea
1.1	colorless, Arkansas, 8051, Lea

CORUNDUM – Ruby

138.7	red (the Rosser Reeves, a star), Sri Lanka, 4257, Reeves
50.3	red violet (a star), Sri Lanka, 173, Lea
33.8	red (a star), Sri Lanka, 1922, Lea

CORUNDUM – Sapphire

423	blue (the Logan), Sri Lanka, 3703, Logan
330	blue (the Star of Asia, a star), Burma, 3688
316	blue (the Star of Artaban, a star), Sri Lanka, 2231, Ingram
98.6	blue (the Bismarck), Sri Lanka, 4753, Bismarck
92.6	yellow, Burma, 3549
67.1	black (a star), Thailand, 4375, Lea
62	dark green (a star), Australia, 4657, Cutter
55	blue, Sri Lanka, 7722, Berry

42.2	purple, Sri Lanka, 4371, Clark
39.8	blue (a star), Sri Lanka, 174, Lea
38.7	green (a star), Australia, 4924, Cutter
35.4	yellow brown, Sri Lanka, 2147, Lea
31	orange, Sri Lanka, 4357, Clark
27.4	violet, Sri Lanka, 4370, Clark
25.9	yellow, Sri Lanka, 4194
25.9	pale yellow, Sri Lanka, 2016, Lea
22.4	yellow orange, Sri Lanka, 3875, Lea
19.9	pink, Sri Lanka, 4372, Clark
18.4	dark blue (a star), Australia, 5278
17	blue, Sri Lanka, 5027, O'Dunne
16.8	green, Burma, 2172, Lea
15.7	pale blue, Sri Lanka, 3581, Lea
15.1	pale orange, Sri Lanka, 3106, Lea
12.8	pink, Sri Lanka, 4373, Clark
12.6	purple, Sri Lanka, 3641
10.2	blue, Montana, 7707

BERYL – Emerald

74	green, Colombia, 7719, Hooker
37.8	green (the Chalk), Colombia, 4931, Chalk
21	green (the Maximilian), Colombia, 5024, Post
17	green (carved), unknown, 3920, MacVeagh
7.1	green, North Carolina, 3075, Lea
6.5	green, North Carolina, 3076, Lea
4.6	green (a cat's eye), Colombia, 2256, Roebling

BERYL – Aquamarine

1000	blue green (the "Most Precious"), Brazil, 3889, Langer
911	blue, Brazil, 4348
263.5	blue, Russia, 3606, Neal
187	blue, Brazil, 3683, Erickson
184	blue green, Brazil, 6186, Harrold
126	blue, Brazil, 4159, Erickson
111.5	blue, Idaho, 5005, Montgomery
71.2	pale blue, Sri Lanka, 3172, Lea
66.3	pale blue green, Maine, 2148, Lea
60	blue (a cat's eye), Sri Lanka, 7479
59.3	blue, Brazil, 4930, Morris
54.6	blue green (a cat's eye), Brazil, 7760, Klein
40.7	blue green, Madagascar, 1871, Lea
22.9	pale blue, Brazil, 7964, Holmes
22.8	pale blue, Brazil, 7966, Holmes
21.2	pale blue, Brazil, 7984-7, Thomas
20.7	pale blue, Madagascar, 1872, Lea
20	pale blue, Brazil, 7984-6, Thomas
19.5	pale blue, Brazil, 7967, Holmes
19.3	pale blue, Brazil, 7967, Holmes
18.9	pale blue, Brazil, 7961, Holmes
18.5	pale blue, Brazil, 7960, Holmes
18.4	pale blue, Brazil, 7959, Holmes
16.2	pale blue, Brazil, 7965, Holmes
15.3	pale blue, Brazil, 7984-5, Thomas
15.3	pale blue, Brazil, 7984-4, Thomas
14.9	pale blue, Brazil, 7963, Holmes
14.7	pale blue, Brazil, 7984-3, Thomas
14.3	blue, Connecticut, 779
10.1	light blue, Kenya, 8085, Dahrling

BERYL – Morganite

330	orange, Brazil, 7759, Klein
235.5	pink, Brazil, 3780, Ix
122.2	pale pink, California, 1988, Lea
113.2	peach, California, 4286, Lea
82.8	pink, Brazil, 5697, Mason
79.6	pale pink, Brazil, 4190, Roebling
69.7	pale pink, Brazil, 5696, Batista
64.1	pink, Brazil, 3721, Roebling
56	pink, Madagascar, 2223, Roebling
24.8	pink, Madagascar, 1976, Lea

BERYL – Other Colors

2054	green gold, Brazil, 3725, Roebling
1363	green, Brazil, 3916
914	green, Brazil, 3919
578	green, Brazil, 3227, Roebling
133.5	yellow, Madagascar, 1977, Lea
98.4	pale green, Brazil, 3949, Cutter
61.9	colorless, Brazil, 3366
47	gold, Brazil, 5699, Johansen
46.4	gold, Madagascar, 2121, Lea
43.5	gold (a cat's eye), Madagascar, 3248
40.4	pale green, Connecticut, 1037, Lea
39.6	yellow green, North Carolina, 2260, Roebling
23	yellow green, Maine, 1031, Lea
21.6	yellow green, Russia, 713
19.8	brown (a star), Brazil, 3355, Lea
17.5	yellow, Russia, 714
14.1	gray (a star), Brazil, 6171, Thornton
12.3	colorless, Russia, 696
9.7	colorless, New Hampshire, 3340, Lea

TOPAZ

12555	yellow green, Brazil, 8053

7725	yellow, Brazil, 3976	17.5	pink (a cat's eye), California, 3786, Lea
3273	blue, Brazil, 3633	15.9	rose, Madagascar, 2135, Lea
2680	colorless, Brazil, 4290, Lea	14.5	pink, California, 3412, Roebling
1469	yellow green, Brazil, 3891		
1300	sherry, Brazil, 6756, Landau		
728	pale sherry, Brazil, 7849, Yampol		
685	pale blue, Brazil, 3003		

TOURMALINE – Other Colors

398	pale blue, Russia, 3400, Roebling
300.6	blue, Brazil, 8113, Kirk
297	smoky, Russia, 5004
234.6	colorless, Colorado, 3309, Lea
227.6	blue, Brazil, 8114, Stornelli
187.2	colorless, Brazil, 3612, Cutter
170.8	champagne, Madagascar, 3890
165	blue, Brazil, 5698, Johansen
155.5	blue, Russia, 262
150.7	deep blue, Brazil, 7758, Sinclair
146.4	pale blue, Texas, 3625, Lea
129	sherry, Brazil, 3550
93.6	orange, Brazil, 3401, Roebling
93	colorless, Nigeria, 7466, Hayes
77.1	yellow, Brazil, 4916, Berman
73.9	blue, Brazil, 8118, Smith
69.5	bi-color, Russia, 8112, Burr
54.4	blue, Brazil, 2219, Lea
50.8	colorless, Japan, 268
50	blue, California, 5668, Van der Velde
43.7	blue, Maine, 2047, Lea
43.5	colorless, unknown, 2155, Lea
41.4	orange, Brazil, 2174, Lea
34.1	gold, Brazil, 2046, Lea
34.1	deep pink, Brazil, 2232, Lea
29	pale yellow, Brazil, 2098, Lea
24.4	pale blue, New Hampshire, 3307, Lea
19.3	colorless, Sri Lanka, 5801, Canfield
18.1	blue, Rhodesia, 4942
18.1	colorless, Japan, 1178
17	blue, California, 3679, Ware
14.6	sherry, Colorado, 318, Lea.

172.7	champagne, Mozambique, 3590, Roebling
124.8	champagne, Mozambique, 3576, Roebling
122.9	green, Mozambique, 3575, Roebling
117.6	pale green, Brazil, 4349
110	green, Brazil, 4197
103.9	rose, Mozambique, 3256, Lea
76	dark green (a cat's eye), Brazil, 3599, Lea
65.5	green (a cat's eye), Brazil, 5700, Stuart
60	blue green, Brazil, 3410, Roebling
58.5	green, Maine, 1108, Lea
53.2	green (a cat's eye), Brazil, 3119, Lea
48	red and green, California, 3363
46	green, Afghanistan, 5015
41.7	yellow, Brazil, 2251, Roebling
40.3	red brown, Brazil, 2097, Roebling
40.3	green, Madagascar, 4081, Roebling
40.3	green, Tanzania, 4935, Lea
36.8	blue green, Brazil, 1118
35.2	dark green, Maine, 8068, Saul
34.3	red brown, Brazil, 2253, Roebling
33.8	rose brown, Brazil, 3428, Roebling
33.4	green (a cat's eye), California, 6815
31.7	pale green, Brazil, 3414, Roebling
31.3	rose brown, Brazil, 3416, Roebling
25.5	blue, Brazil, 3298, Roebling
23.5	pale brown, Brazil, 3417, Roebling
21.1	yellow green, Maine, 4621, Lea
20.9	dark green, unknown, 8073, Saul
20.4	blue green, Madagascar, 2032, Lea
18	green, Brazil, 2142, Lea
17.9	green, South Africa, 2095, Lea
17.8	brown, Brazil, 2154, Lea
17.7	yellow green, Italy, 3368, Roebling
17	green, Maine, 1955, Lea
15.1	pale green, Brazil, 3413, Roebling
14.7	yellow, Brazil, 3415, Roebling

TOURMALINE – Rubellite

246	pink (faceted egg), California, 7717
116.2	rose, California, 8110, Putterman
110.8	red, Manchuria, 3173, Roebling
100	pink, California, 8137, Dahrling
75	rosy red, Brazil, 8129, Chiu
62.4	pink, Brazil, 3411, Roebling
50.5	magenta, Brazil, 4160, Erickson
35.3	pink, Brazil, 2254, Roebling
30	pink, Madagascar, 3409, Roebling
28.2	red, Brazil, 4358, Clark
19.2	rose, Brazil, 2143
18.8	rose, Madagascar, 4196, Lea
18.4	pink, Maine, 1109, Lea

TOURMALINE – Uvite

- 41.6 brown, Sri Lanka, 3245, Lea
- 2.1 smoky yellow, Sri Lanka, 6270, Bosch

SPINEL

- 45.8 pale purple, Sri Lanka, 2180, Lea
- 36.1 indigo, Burma, 3685
- 34 red, Burma, 3354, Lea
- 30 violet, Burma, 3344, Lea
- 29.7 purple, Sri Lanka, 2165, Lea
- 25.5 blue gray, Burma, 3593, Lea
- 22.2 rose brown, Sri Lanka, 2166, Lea
- 22.1 blue violet, Sri Lanka, 2247, Roebling
- 13.7 mauve, Sri Lanka, 2138, Lea
- 10.2 red, Burma, 2141, Lea
- 8.3 pink, unknown, 2242, Roebling
- 6.6 black (a star), Sri Lanka, 2255, Roebling

ZIRCON

- 118.1 brown, Sri Lanka, 2236, Roebling
- 105.9 brown, Thailand, 3568
- 103.2 blue, Thailand, 2222, Roebling
- 97.6 yellow brown, Sri Lanka, 2237, Roebling
- 75.8 red brown, Burma, 3068, Lea
- 64.2 brown, Thailand, 3397, Roebling
- 51.3 brown, Sri Lanka, 1179, Lea
- 48.2 colorless, Sri Lanka, 3554, Lea
- 43.9 pale brown, Sri Lanka, 2235, Roebling
- 29.2 blue, Thailand, 3394, Roebling
- 28.1 brown, Thailand, 2173, Lea
- 23.9 colorless, Sri Lanka, 2234, Roebling
- 23.5 green, Sri Lanka, 2233, Roebling
- 22.4 brown, Thailand, 2224, Roebling
- 21.2 green, Sri Lanka, 325
- 21.2 tan, Australia, 1887, Lea
- 11.3 green, Sri Lanka, 2152
- 10.9 blue, Thailand, 1861, Lea

SPODUMENE – Kunzite

- 880 violet, Brazil, 3940
- 336.2 violet, Brazil, 3942
- 296.8 violet, Brazil, 3941
- 287.7 mauve, Brazil, 6187, Harrold
- 177 violet, California, 3797, Am. Gem. Soc.
- 116 magenta, Brazil, 8116, Malone

- 75.9 pale pink, California, 1914, Lea
- 63 pale pink, Brazil, 3684
- 60.7 pale pink, California, 1915, Lea
- 51 light lavender, Afghanistan, 8124, Hawks
- 36.3 pale pink, California, 3226, Roebling
- 24.7 pale violet, Madagascar, 1979, Lea
- 11.6 pale pink, North Carolina, 3395, Roebling

SPODUMENE – Other Colors

- 327 yellow, Brazil, 3396, Roebling
- 255.8 yellow, Brazil, 3429, Roebling
- 71.1 yellow, Madagascar, 3698, Lea
- 68.8 yellow green, Brazil, 3885, Roebling
- 44.9 yellow, Brazil, 2163, Lea
- 35.3 white (a cat's eye), Maine, 3244
- 24.7 yellow, Madagascar, 2261, Canfield

PERIDOT

- 310 olive green, Egypt, 3398, Roebling
- 287 olive green, Burma, 3705
- 103.3 olive green, unknown, 7882, Dubin
- 45.5 olive green, Egypt, 1978, Lea
- 22.9 olive green, Arizona, 3620, Lea
- 12 green (a star), Burma, 3347
- 11 green, Arizona, 8131, Lauer
- 10.4 green, Egypt, 1924, Lea
- 8.9 olive green, Arizona, 1925, Lea
- 8.6 green, Arizona, 3339, Lea

GARNET – Almandine

- 174 red (a star), Idaho, 3670
- 57.5 red brown, India, 833
- 40.6 red brown, Madagascar, 2137, Lea
- 25.7 red brown, Idaho, 3423, Lea
- 24.4 red brown, India, 834

GARNET – Andradite

- 10.4 green (demantoid), Russia, 2175
- 4.1 green (demantoid), Russia, 2150, Lea
- 3.4 green (demantoid), Russia, 3627
- 3.2 green (demantoid), Russia, 142
- 2.3 green (demantoid), Russia, 141

GARNET – Grossular

9.2	yellow orange, Sri Lanka, 2246, Roebling
6.3	green (tsavorite), Kenya, 8087, Dahrling

GARNET – Rhodolite

74.3	purple, Tanzania, 4806, Saul
22.1	rose violet, Tanzania, 4080, Lea
16.5	red, North Carolina, 4361, Clark
6.4	violet, North Carolina, 460, Lea

GARNET – Spessartine

109	red, Brazil, 4203
54	red, Brazil, 3229, Lea
40.1	orange, Virginia, 147, Lea
26.3	orange, Virginia, 3597, Lea
11.8	orange, Virginia, 152, Lea

QUARTZ – Amethyst

1362	purple, Brazil, 3879
202.5	pale lavender, North Carolina, 1286, Lea
182.6	purple, Brazil, 1272, Lea
96	purple, Brazil, 5273, Morris
67	purple, Brazil, 7986-41, Thomas
61.4	purple, Brazil, 3914, Cutter
56	purple, Brazil, 3165, Capps
55.9	purple, Brazil, 7986-40, Thomas
53.7	purple, Pennsylvania, 1299, Lea.
53.4	purple, Brazil, 7986-39, Thomas
48.8	purple, Brazil, 7986-38, Thomas
44.5	pale purple, North Carolina, 1298, Lea
41.2	purple, Brazil, 4355, Clark
38.9	purple, 7986-37, Thomas
38	purple, Brazil, 7986-47, Thomas
36.2	purple, Pennsylvania, 1283, Lea
33.2	pale purple, North Carolina, 1288, Lea.
29.7	purple, Brazil, 3166, Capps
29.2	purple, Brazil, 7986-46, Thomas
27.9	purple, Brazil, 7986-45, Thomas
27.5	purple, North Carolina, 1289, Lea
24.9	purple, Brazil, 7986-44, Thomas
24.5	purple, Brazil, 7986-43, Thomas
24.2	purple, Japan, 1281
22.9	purple, Maine, 1271, Lea
22.6	purple, Brazil, 4356, Clark
22.6	purple, Brazil, 7986-42, Thomas
21.4	purple, Brazil, 7986-36, Thomas
21.3	purple, unknown, 1303
18.7	purple, Virginia, 1301, Lea
15.9	banded, unknown, 8143, Lea

QUARTZ – Citrine

1180	golden brown, Brazil, 1870, Lea
783	pale golden brown, Brazil, 3640
640	yellow brown, Brazil, 7721, Ashley
469	yellow brown, Brazil, 8127, Kupper
277.9	golden brown, Brazil, 3732, Cutter
264.8	pale golden brown, Brazil, 2041, Roebling
226.9	pale yellow, Brazil, 3718, Cutter
217.5	golden brown, Brazil, 4199, Cutter
189.3	yellow, Brazil, 7473, Hurlburt
169	golden brown, Australia, 1373, Lea
159	pale yellow, Brazil, 1310
155.7	yellow brown, Brazil, 1311, Lea
150	yellow, Brazil, 1980, Lea
143.3	yellow, Colorado, 456, Lea
120.3	golden brown, Brazil, 2116, Lea
114.6	golden brown, Brazil, 3932
101	yellow brown, Brazil, 8080, Dahrling
99.6	pale yellow, Sri Lanka, 1372, Lea
97	pale yellow, Sri Lanka, 1344, Lea
95.6	yellow brown, Brazil, 2193
91.9	yellow, Brazil, 1331
90.5	yellow, Brazil, 3615, Cutter
87.5	yellow, Brazil, 4915, Mason
78.8	pale yellow, Brazil, 3621, Cutter
69.5	yellow, Brazil, 4288, Hurlburt
66	sherry, unknown, 3169, Capps
61.1	yellow, Brazil, 2273
59.3	brown yellow, Brazil, 1312
58.3	yellow, unknown, 1360
55	pale golden brown, Maine, 2178, Lea
54.6	yellow, Brazil, 1313
48.4	yellow, Brazil, 3915, Cutter
47.2	yellow brown, Brazil, 2275
45.8	pale yellow, Brazil, 8078, Dahrling
43.1	yellow brown, Brazil, 2270
42.8	yellow, Brazil, 3719, Cutter
42.3	yellow, Brazil, 2272
38.9	yellow, Brazil, 2269
35	pale yellow, Brazil, 1314
34.4	yellow brown, Brazil, 2276
34.3	pale yellow, unknown, 1361
33.3	pale yellow, unknown, 1315
30.6	yellow, unknown, 6155, Lea
29.4	pale yellow, unknown, 1363
28.1	yellow, Brazil, 2268
26.4	yellow, unknown, 3168, Capps
25.2	yellow brown, Brazil, 1318
22	yellow, Brazil, 2277
21.3	yellow, unknown, 1364

QUARTZ – Rock Crystal

7000	colorless, Brazil, 3957, Lea
654	colorless, Brazil, 5701, West
625	colorless (a star), New Hampshire, 3125, Burroughs
357.9	colorless, Brazil, 4205, Int. Imp. Co.
355.6	colorless, Brazil, 4204, Int. Imp. Co.
353.6	colorless, North Carolina, 1397, Lea
350.1	colorless, North Carolina, 1398, Lea.
270	gray (a star), unknown, 8111, Turetsky
235	colorless, Brazil, 8128, Kupper

QUARTZ – Rose Quartz

625	pink (a star sphere), Brazil, 4264, Hueber
375	pink, Brazil, 3592, Lea
84	pink, Brazil, 3421
48.8	pink, Brazil, 3420, Roebling
46.4	pink, Brazil, 3336
43.5	pink, Sri Lanka, 1267
30.4	pink, Brazil, 4807, Mitchell
27.9	pink, Brazil, 4911, Wyka
21.8	pink, South Dakota, 4510, Jameson
20.9	pink, Brazil, 4912, Bruce
18.4	pink, France, 1266, Seaman
15.8	pink, Germany, 1269
13.4	pink, Germany, 1268
10	pink, South Dakota, 3722, Lea

QUARTZ – Smoky Quartz

4500	pale smoky, California, 3738, Lea
1695	smoky, Brazil, 3697, Lea
785	pale smoky, Colorado, 1335, Lea
543.2	pale smoky, North Carolina, 1339, Lea
284.1	pale smoky, North Carolina, 1340, Lea
268.5	pale smoky, Switzerland, 1348
163.4	pale smoky, Colorado, 1336, Lea
144.9	smoky, Scotland, 3079, Roebling
128.1	smoky, Sri Lanka, 1343, Lea
90	dark smoky, Switzerland, 3293
80	smoky, Arkansas, 1334
63	smoky, Maine, 1338
35.1	smoky, Scotland, 1374
32	smoky, New Hampshire, 3124, Burroughs
28.9	smoky, Brazil, 2271

QUARTZ – Greened Amethyst

22.3	green, Brazil, 3296, Lea

CHRYSOBERYL – Alexandrite

65.7	green to red, Sri Lanka, 2042, Lea
16.7	green to red, Sri Lanka, 3407, Roebling
10	green to red, Sri Lanka, 6760, Johnson

CHRYSOBERYL – Other Colors

171.5	gray green (a cat's eye), Sri Lanka, 3924
120.5	green, Sri Lanka, 3001, Roebling
114.3	yellow green, Brazil, 4905
58.2	green (the Maharani, a cat's eye), Sri Lanka, 3642
46.3	green yellow, Brazil, 1923, Lea
31.7	brown, Sri Lanka, 2151, Lea
14	smoky yellow, Brazil, 2184
13.8	yellow green, Brazil, 2250, Roebling
8.5	yellow brown, Sri Lanka, 555, Lea
6.7	dark green (a star), Brazil, 3680, Ware

OPAL

355	black with fire, Nevada, 3969, Roebling
345	white with fire, Australia, 4585, Everhart
162	white with fire, Australia, 8125, Mosmann
155	white with fire, Australia, 3285, Roebling
146	white with fire, Australia, 6763, Penner
143	orange with fire, Mexico, 3968
105	white with fire, Australia, 6761, Penner
90	white with fire, Australia, 6762, Penner
83	white with fire, Australia, 3300, Roebling
65.5	orange brown, Mexico, 8115, De Leo
58.8	black with fire, Australia, 3960, Roebling
55.9	colorless with fire, Mexico, 2240, Roebling
54.3	black with fire, Australia, 3962, Roebling
44	black with fire, Australia, 3284, Roebling

39	pale yellow orange with fire, Brazil, 3637
38.8	orange, Mexico, 8081, Dahrling
38.3	black with fire, Australia, 3961, Roebling
34.4	orange, Brazil, 3696
30.1	black with fire, Australia, 3405, Roebling
29.9	orange, Mexico, 5393
26.9	black with fire, Australia, 8109, Cowger
26.4	white with fire, Mexico, 3571
25.3	orange, Mexico, 8072, Saul
24.3	black with fire, Australia, 1897, Lea
21.8	orange with fire, Mexico, 2028, Lea
21.6	orange with fire, Mexico, 2106, Lea
21.4	yellow with fire, Mexico, 2111, Lea
20	colorless with fire, Mexico, 461
19.4	white with fire, Australia, 6764, Penner
18.9	pale yellow with fire, Brazil, 3228, Lea
16.6	black with fire, Nevada, 1084, Lea
16.5	white with fire, Australia, 6765, Penner
16	colorless with fire, Mexico, 8042, Lea
15.1	orange with fire, Mexico, 2096
14.9	colorless with fire, Mexico, 2113, Lea
14.5	colorless with fire, Mexico, 1072, Lea
12.5	colorless with fire, Mexico, 1069
11.8	pale yellow with fire, Mexico, 2112, Lea
11.5	orange with fire, Mexico, 3886, Lewis

OTHER LESS–KNOWN SPECIES

ALBITE

42.6	white (a cat's eye), Burma, 3311, Lea

AMBLYGONITE

62.5	yellow, Brazil, 4079, Lea
57.8	yellow, Brazil, 8241, Zajicek
39.6	yellow, Brazil, 8058, Saul
19.7	yellow, Burma, 3562, Roebling
9.9	pale yellow, Brazil, 7922

ANDALUSITE

30.4	brown, Brazil, 4939
28.3	brown, Brazil, 3619, Kennedy
13.5	green brown, Brazil, 3364, Lea

ANGLESITE

77.5	gold, Southwest Africa, 5706
8.9	colorless, Southwest Africa, 5298, Lea
7.6	amber, Southwest Africa, 5117

ANORTHITE

5.6	pale yellow, Alaska, 7916, Hoover
4.2	pale yellow, Alaska, 7917, Hoover

APATITE

51.4	green, Mexico, 4943
46.2	green (a cat's eye), Brazil, 7726, Bagchi
29	yellow, Mexico, 3594, Lea
28.8	yellow green, Burma, 3247, Lea
19.8	yellow, Mexico, 3570
14.7	colorless, Burma, 3720, Roebling
13.9	yellow, Mexico, 2218
11.1	yellow, Mexico, 2217
9.6	green, Brazil, 4949, Berman
9	yellow green, Canada, 3122, Roebling
8.8	pale blue, Sri Lanka, 3639
7.7	pale green, California, 3636
5.4	green, Madagascar, 3676, Durand

APOPHYLLITE

15.4	colorless, India, 5395

ARAGONITE

4.2	colorless, Czechoslovakia, 3252

AUGELITE

2.4	colorless, California, 8100, Stornelli
1.5	colorless, California, 7923, Roth

AXINITE

23.6	brown, Mexico, 4289, Roebling

9.4	brown, Mexico, 37.87, Roebling	
9	brown, Mexico, 3773, Lea	
1.6	brown, France, 581	

BARITE

97	colorless, England, 8117, Roth
64.8	colorless, Colorado, 8062, Saul
60.7	colorless, England, 3349

BENITOITE

7.6	blue, California, 3387, Roebling
1.1	blue, California, 4506
1	blue, California, 4174, Lea

BERYLLONITE

5	colorless, Maine, 423
3.9	colorless, Maine, 424

BRAZILIANITE

41.9	yellow, Brazil, 3083, Lea
17	yellow, Brazil, 3788, Roebling

BYTOWNITE

1.7	red, Oregon, 2114, Lea

CALCITE

474	pale yellow, Russia, 8126, Krotki
173	pale yellow, Mexico, 6812, Swabe
104.3	pale yellow, unknown, 8084, Dahrling
75.8	gold brown, Mexico, 4583, Roebling
70.5	pale yellow, unknown, 8060, Saul
70	red amber, Mexico, 7910, Leader
45.8	gold brown, Mexico, 3305

CASSITERITE

10	yellow brown, Bolivia, 3250

CERUSSITE

109.9	smoky, Southwest Africa, 8059, Saul
4.7	pale yellow, Southwest Africa, 3234, Roebling

COBALTIAN CALCITE

3.9	pink, Spain, 4176, Lea
3.3	pink, Spain, 3724, Lea

COLEMANITE

14.9	colorless, California, 4941

CORDIERITE

15.6	blue, Sri Lanka, 3882
10.2	indigo, Sri Lanka, 3580, Lea
9.4	blue, Sri Lanka, 3881

CROCOITE

5.7	orange red, Australia, 8139, DeBoer

CUPRITE

203	deep red, Southwest Africa, 8122, Whitely
172	deep red, Southwest Africa, 5705
125.5	deep red, Southwest Africa, 8057, Saul
110	deep red, Southwest Africa, 8082, Dahrling

DANBURITE

18.4	yellow, Burma, 3345, Lea
12.4	colorless, Mexico, 7737, Stornelli
10.5	colorless, Mexico, 6179, Smith
7.9	colorless, Japan, 3081, Lea
6.4	colorless, Japan, 3074, D'Ascenzo

DATOLITE

5.4	colorless, Massachusetts, 3876, Boucot
5	colorless, Massachusetts, 3283, Sinkankas

DIOPSIDE

132.5	black (a star), India, 3977
24	black (a cat's eye), India, 3956, Lea
19.2	green, Madagascar, 4504, Roebling

15.6	green, Madagascar, 4505, Roebling
14	black (a cat's eye), India, 3880
10	black (a star), India, 4353, Int. Imp. Co.
8.6	green, New York, 4936
6.8	yellow, Italy, 3634
5.6	black (a cat's eye), India, 3873, Int. Imp. Co.
4.6	yellow, Burma, 3346, Lea
1.6	green (chrome diopside), Finland, 3693
1.2	yellow green, unknown, 578

ENSTATITE

11	brown, Sri Lanka, 3638
8.1	brown, Sri Lanka, 2294, Roebling
7.8	brown, Tanzania, 5707

EPIDOTE

3.9	brown, Austria, 579

EUCLASE

12.5	green, Brazil, 3214, Roebling
8.9	yellow, Brazil, 3215, Roebling
8.9	yellow, Brazil, 2181, Lea
7.7	colorless, Brazil, 8071, Saul
3.7	blue green, Brazil, 3388, Roebling

FLUORITE

729.3	green, Colombia, 8105, Bhat
492.1	pink, Korea, 7905, Gratz
354.4	pink, Korea, 7907, Gratz
354	pale yellow, Illinois, 3877
348.3	pale blue, Korea, 7906, Gratz
263.6	light brown, Africa, 8102, Bhat
234.6	light brown, Africa, 8094, Caldwell
229.3	light green, New Hampshire, 8096, Caldwell
203.4	brownish rose, England, 8108, Bagchi
124.5	green, New Hampshire, 3294
118.7	purple, England, 8098, Caldwell
118.5	blue, Illinois, 8101, Bhat
117	green, Africa, 2153
111.2	violet, Illinois, 4270
107.8	pink, Mexico, 7837
105.4	purple, Spain, 8095, Caldwell
105.3	colorless, Colombia, 8089, Caldwell
104.3	yellow, Illinois, 4268
99.7	purple, South Africa, 8106, Kawaoka
94.8	green, Africa, 8093, Caldwell
86.9	blue, Illinois, 4875
83	smoky rose, Korea, 8140, Tepper
69.3	green and white, Colombia, 8103, Bhat
63	yellow, Illinois, 3595, Lea
57.8	blue, South Africa, 4934, Roebling
52.7	olive, Canada, 8092, Caldwell
52.6	green, South Africa, 7911, Leader
49.4	green, Colombia, 4945
46.9	yellow, Illinois, 5394
39.7	yellow, England, 7908, Gratz
35.6	lavender, Illinois, 8097, Caldwell
35.1	green, Colombia, 5114
33.3	brown green, Brazil, 8091, Caldwell
33.2	pale green, Colombia, 8088, Caldwell
32.7	colorless, Illinois, 3626
27.2	green, France, 8090, Caldwell
24.2	purple, New York, 8104, Bhat
17.5	yellow, Illinois, 3635
17.2	bicolor, Illinois, 7909, Gratz
16	green, Canada, 8107, Kawaoka
13.9	peach, England, 7727, Bagchi
13	pink, Switzerland, 4434, Canfield
9.6	colorless, unknown, 2290, Paskow
8	pink, Switzerland, 3730, Roebling
6.1	purple brown, Virginia, 8099, Caldwell

FRIEDELITE

11.8	red brown, New Jersey, 3013, D'Ascenzo

GADOLINITE

8.6	black, Texas, 587, Lea

GAHNITE

2.2	green, Brazil, 3553, Romanella

HAMBURGITE

2.9	colorless, Madagascar, 7838
2.6	colorless, Madagascar, 7840
2.4	colorless, Madagascar, 7841
2.1	colorless, Madagascar, 7839
1.4	colorless, Madagascar, 7842
1.2	colorless, Madagascar, 7847

HEMIMORPHITE

- 2.5 colorless, Mexico, 4816

HYDROXYL HERDERITE

- 5.9 pale green, Brazil, 4948
- 2.1 blue gray, Brazil, 8070, Saul

JEREMEJEVITE

- 1.4 pale blue, Southwest Africa, 5693

KORNERUPINE

- 21.6 brown, Sri Lanka, 3706, Lea
- 10.8 brown, Madagascar, 3567, Lea
- 8.1 green brown, Sri Lanka, 3390, Roebling
- 7.6 green, Madagascar, 3782

KYANITE

- 10.9 blue, Brazil, 7924, Roth
- 10.7 blue, Brazil, 3557, Lea
- 9.1 green, Brazil, 3558, Lea
- 4.9 blue, Tanzania, 4508, Lea
- 3.7 blue, North Carolina, 564, Bowman

LABRADORITE

- 30 pale yellow, Idaho, 5703, Lea
- 11.1 pale yellow, Utah, 3121
- 5.8 pale yellow, Nevada, 2115, Lea

LEGRANDITE

- 1.1 yellow, Mexico, 4933

MAGNESITE

- 134.5 colorless, Brazil, 8121, Tan
- 23.1 colorless, Brazil, 8061, Saul

MICROLITE

- 3.7 brown, Virginia, 3588, Lea

NATROLITE

- 9.3 colorless, New Jersey, 5111
- 7.9 colorless, New Jersey, 5116
- 3.7 colorless, California, 7912, Leader
- 1.4 colorless, California, 4352, Lea

OLIGOCLASE

- 6 colorless, North Carolina, 404, Lea

ORTHOCLASE

- 249.6 yellow, Madagascar, 3878
- 104.5 pale green (a cat's eye), Sri Lanka, 3883
- 61 yellow, Madagascar, 1838, Lea
- 30.5 colorless, Madagascar, 7925 Roth
- 25.9 gray (a cat's eye), Sri Lanka, 3579, Lea
- 22.7 white (a star), Sri Lanka, 3578, Lea
- 18 colorless, Madagascar, 1820, Lea
- 17.2 colorless, unknown, 8066, Saul
- 16.4 yellow, Madagascar, 3393, Roebling

PETALITE

- 55 colorless, Southwest Africa, 4222, Lea
- 48.3 colorless, Brazil, 8138, De Beer
- 45.9 colorless, Brazil, 8120, Decosimo
- 26.6 colorless, Brazil, 8083, Dahrling
- 19.7 colorless, Brazil, 8069, Saul
- 10.7 colorless, Southwest Africa, 3096

PHENACITE

- 22.2 colorless, Russia, 3739
- 21.9 colorless, Brazil, 4938
- 6.4 colorless, Brazil, 7833, Burr
- 5.2 colorless, Russia, 830, Lea
- 5 colorless, Brazil, 7926, Roth

PHOSPHOPHYLLITE

- 26.9 green, Bolivia, Korfmacher
- 5 green, Bolivia, 3950, Roebling
- 4 green, Bolivia, 4944

POLLUCITE

- 8.5 colorless, Maine, 2056, Lea
- 7 colorless, Connecticut, 3802, Roebling

PREHNITE

    4.4   yellow green, Scotland, 4376, Lea

PROUSTITE

    9.9   red, Germany, 4082

RHODIZITE

    .5   colorless, Madagascar, 3219, Canfield

RHODOCHROSITE

    20.8   red, South Africa, 4920
    15.2   red, South Africa, 4940
    11.3   rose, Argentina, 8065, Saul
    9.5   red, South Africa, 4189, Roebling
    2.2   rose pink, Colorado, 8133, Lauer

SAMARSKITE

    6.6   black, North Carolina, 588, Lea

SCAPOLITE

    288   colorless (meionite), Burma 3783
    103.4   yellow (marialite), Tanzania, 7348
    52.2   yellow, Tanzania, 7929, Stange
    29.9   colorless (a cat's eye), Burma, 3301, Lea
    21.5   pale yellow, Tanzania, 8063, Saul
    19.7   colorless (a cat's eye), Burma, 3561, Ehrmann
    19.7   yellow, Tanzania, 8064, Saul
    17.3   pink (a cat's eye, marialite), Sri Lanka, 3238, Roebling
    12.3   pink (marialite), Burma, 3674, Lea
    8.2   colorless (marialite), Madagascar, 1818, Lea

SCORODITE

    2.6   purple, Southwest Africa, 3793

SILLIMANITE

    5.9   black (a cat's eye), South Carolina, 3600, Lea

SINHALITE

    109.8   brown, Sri Lanka, 3587

    43.5   brown, Sri Lanka, 3548, Lea
    36.4   brown, Sri Lanka, 8130, Chiu

SMITHSONITE

    2.7   pale yellow, Southwest Africa, 8076, Dahrling

SODALITE

    8.7   blue, unknown, 6180, Lea

SPHALERITE

    73.3   yellow brown, Utah, 3556
    68.9   yellow brown, Utah, 3362
    61.9   yellow brown, Spain, 8055, Saul
    59.5   yellow green, New Jersey, 3874, Roebling
    48   yellow, Mexico, 2167, Lea
    45.9   yellow, Spain, 3707, Lea
    36.6   yellow green, Spain, 8056, Saul
    18.5   yellow brown, Utah, 3555, Lea

SPHENE

    .8–.93   gold (matched set 16 stones), Switzerland, 2043, Lea
    8.5   brown, New York, 550
    5.6   yellow brown, Mexico, 3290, Roebling
    5.2   yellow brown, Mexico, 3292, Lea
    4.3   green brown, Pennsylvania, 552, Forwood

STAUROLITE

    3   red brown, Brazil, 3795

STIBIOTANTALITE

    7.3   yellow, Brazil, 4917, Lea
    2.5   brown, Mozambique, 3218, Canfield

TAAFFEITE

    5.3   mauve, Sri Lanka, 4509, Kennedy

TEKTITE

    23   brown (moldavite), Czechoslovakia, 681, Lea

TREMOLITE

    .4   rose (hexagonite), New York, 3242

VESUVIANITE

  7.1   brown, Tanzania, 4937, Lea
  3.5   brown, Italy, 4179, Roebling
  2.3   green brown, Italy, 3392, Roebling

WILLEMITE

 11.7   orange yellow, New Jersey, 1898, Lea
 11.1   orange yellow, New Jersey, 4187, Lea

WULFENITE

 46.1   pale yellow, Southwest Africa, 8067, Saul
 15.7   yellow, Southwest Africa, 7826
  9.6   yellow, Southwest Africa, 5118
  3.7   colorless, Southwest Africa, 5119

ZINCITE

 20.1   red, New Jersey, 3386, Roebling
 12.3   red, New Jersey, 3002, Roebling

ZOISITE

122.7   blue (tanzanite), Tanzania, 4876
 18.2   blue (tanzanite, a cat's eye), Tanzania, 4584, Lea

Paul E. Desautels is a fellow of the Mineralogical Society of America and an honorary member of the American Gem Society and several gem and mineral societies across the United States. In addition to many scientific and popular articles and books, he has written two widely read "companion" books, *The Gem Kingdom* and *The Mineral Kingdom*.

This book was produced by the Smithsonian Institution Press, Washington, D.C. Printed by Printing Service Company, Dayton, Ohio. Set in Helvetica Light and Eurostyle Bold by Carver Photocomposition, Inc. The text paper is seventy-pound Flokote Text with one-hundred pound Coronation cover. Designed by Natalie Babson.